Plan A

Abide in Christ, Disciple the World!

Mike Shipman

Plan A: Abide in Christ, Disciple the World!

Unless otherwise indicated, all Bible quotations are taken from the Updated New American Standard, © Foundation Publications, Inc. Used by permission

ISBN: 978-1-7337618-1-9

Cover design: Caleb Shipman

Published in collaboration with:
The Mission Network
17110 Brook Ct.
Mount Vernon, WA 98274
360 420-5634
TheMissionNetwork.org

Printed in the United States

PLAN A is humbly dedicated to the Savior, who in His infinite wisdom authored our salvation and revealed the flawless plan to disciple the whole world through flawed but redeemed people, empowered by His Spirit.

This book is further dedicated to brothers and sisters worldwide who take up the cross daily and follow Jesus for the sake of discipling all ethnic groups.

Acknowledgements

I praise God for those who've walked with me, going against the flow, to reform modern-day mission practices to reflect the post-Pentecost pattern of Acts. Their lives, like mine, are being transformed through radical Great Commission obedience as they work with the Savior to transform the lives of others.

My wife Kathy has supported me unconditionally through the highs and lows of facilitating a Church Planting Movement and the winding road that led to publication of *Plan A*.

Finally, I want to thank the many people who have given input into the *Plan A* manuscript. Leslie Holzmann, James Hamilton and Caleb Shipman worked countless hours to edit and format the final manuscript of the book. Special thanks also to Robby Butler, who has seen *Plan A* through to publication.

Contents

Foreword

It has been nearly 20 centuries since the Lord gave His commission to a small band of followers on a hill outside of Jerusalem. In sending eleven disciples to engage all the world's *ethne*, Jesus was either delusional, or His instruction carried the genius of multiplication. When coupled with the assurance of His authority and presence, Jesus' commission provided all that was needed for all disciples, all *ethne* and all time.

After 20 centuries of Great Commission effort and innovation, confusion in the task or potential drift from the original message would be understandable. Perhaps this is why God inspired and preserved a record of the means and methods of the mission He has ordained for His Church and their "sent-ones." It is necessary therefore, for each generation to revisit the Lord's command and the example of His first disciples' obedience lest the extra-biblical structures and expectations of Christendom redefine obedience to the final words of the Lord of our faith.

To be sure, 21st century efforts toward addition have proven insufficient for engaging a population that continues to multiply. The western church seems to have fallen in love with professional ministry. Church history has demonstrated, again and again, that where such a pattern usurps an every-member ministry, the church loses ground amidst a multiplying population. Perhaps the time has come for a re-reading of the original instructions.

Mike Shipman points out that our savior was, in fact, a genius. The impossible task of eleven men discipling all the nations requires that we surrender strategy and methods to His simple instruction. Mike reminds us that Jesus' Great Commission is as simple as 1...2...3, yet inherent in the Lord's instruction are all the ingredients necessary for orthodoxy (theological fidelity) as well as orthopraxy (methodological fidelity).

One imperative, two assurances and three tasks that, wherever employed, result in a multiplied work force. As it was applied in the first century, by first disciples, so it is being applied to the end of time, among every *ethne*.

Simple instruction, proven tools, faith for a sure future and passion for the task—any of these would make this book worth your time.

Mike Shipman has provided all of them in this one short volume.

—Nathan Shank
September, 2018

Introduction

It's hard to envision what we've never seen. When my wife and I answered the call to plant churches in a large unreached area, I knew we had to do something different, but I didn't know exactly what that would look like. At the time, all I could picture were the multitudes of lost and perishing people I saw day after day. At first, I couldn't imagine how churches would form among the different kinds of people in the various places where they lived.

Acts gave me a picture for what we wanted to see happen. Applying the discipleship pattern implemented by the apostolic teams and first-century believers of Acts has enabled us to experience a discipleship re-en-Act-ment, resulting in thousands of multiplying churches among the various kinds of people in the area. Now we can clearly see the power and possibilities of applying the first-century discipleship model to the 21st century world. As we've studied the Scripture, abided in Christ and applied original Great Commission principles, we've awakened to the potential of discipling the whole world.

Look Behind You

Are you looking forward to the discovery of a new plan, one that would lead all receptive people in the world to Christ and then disciple them? Look no farther! The secret is behind us. The ageless worldwide discipleship plan was disclosed by Christ about 2,000 years ago. It was demonstrated by first century believers in Acts and described throughout the New Testament, resulting in receptive peoples of the first-century world being discipled. And it still works today—if we apply the original plan! We don't have to create a new plan; all we must do to disciple every kind of people in the world is live by Christ's Spirit and obey the original Great Commission as it was implemented in Acts.

The Great Commission was given by the Lord Jesus Christ to His followers after He was raised from the dead:

> And Jesus came up and spoke to them, saying, "All authority has been given to Me in heaven and on earth. Go therefore and make disciples of all the nations, baptizing them in the name of the Father and the Son and the Holy Spirit, teaching them to observe all that I commanded you; and lo, I am with you always, even to the end of the age" (Matt. 28:18-29).

The word translated here as "nations" is actually *ethnê*, meaning people groups—peoples with a unique ethnic background, culture and/ or language—rather than the political entities we now call "nations." Our English word "ethnic" comes from this Greek term.

Look What Happened After the Spirit Came

Plan A relies on Acts as an inspired account of how the Great Commission was implemented after the promised Holy Spirit came at Pentecost. Acts demonstrates the post-Pentecost mission strategy, and the epistles of the New Testament describe it further. The historical event of Acts can't be replicated, however, the distinctives of the discipleship pattern of Acts should shape and correct our modern mission strategies.

The Acts plan necessarily confronts and corrects the way we usually understand evangelism, discipleship and church planting. *Plan A* will at times expose our prideful attempts to update the original Great Commission and our faulty biblical interpretation of applying pre-Pentecost concepts to post-Pentecost discipleship. It will also challenge us to evaluate our complicated modern methods of discipleship in light of the radical simplicity of first-century ones.

See the Potential of Applying the Whole Great Commission

The next person you lead to Christ could be uniquely prepared by God to form a church—or perhaps to reach and disciple many people who themselves start churches. The new believers who form these churches together become obedient disciples, while reaching out to others in different communities, or even among different people groups—people outside the reach of existing churches. In this way, everyone, in every place, can hear the gospel. Those who receive Christ become churches, creating a community where they can grow to become mature disciples. That's the Great Commission plan, plain and simple. That's *Plan A*, the way the Great Commission was obeyed in Acts. If we follow the model of the apostolic teams of Acts, discipling every believer as a partner in obeying the worldwide discipleship plan, we (led by the Holy Spirit) could disciple the entire world.

Only when we implement Christ's plan, rather than our own, will we experience His power and the fulfillment of His promises. Listen as the Scripture speaks. Learn what the Savior is saying. And let the Spirit guide you in experiencing the greater works of Christ.

All of us can experience the joy of Christ's presence and power as we obediently venture forth on mission with Him. Are you tired of hearing that everyone should obey the Great Commission, yet not knowing how to do it? This book will show you how to do more than witness. You could start a multiplying, generational church movement.

Part One: Envisioning *Plan A*

1. It Could Happen Through You

The Great Commission Made Simple Again

In Revelation, we see the final result of the Great Commission:

> After these things I looked, and behold, a great multitude which no one could count, from every nation and all tribes and peoples and tongues, standing before the throne and before the Lamb, clothed in white robes, and palm branches were in their hands; and they cry out with a loud voice, saying, "Salvation to our God who sits on the throne, and to the Lamb" (Rev. 7:9–10).

How will this happen? For more than 2,000 years, God has worked in various ways to communicate the gospel and build His church through obedience to the Great Commission—even though that obedience was often only partial obedience. However, *finishing* the task will require our full obedience.

The Plan Foretold

Before His sacrificial atonement, Jesus spoke to His disciples in the Upper Room (John 13–17). His time with them was used to prepare them (and all who would believe through their word) to glorify God, by abiding in Christ to fulfill the Great Commission.

Jesus made this God-sized promise to all who would believe and abide in Him: "Truly, truly, I say to you, he who believes in Me, the works that I do, he will do also; and greater works than these he will do, because I go to the Father" (John 14:12). The greater works promised by the Savior refer to the fruit of Great Commission obedience after the Spirit came at Pentecost. This is in accordance with Jesus last earthly statement to them: "But you will receive power when the Holy Spirit has come upon you; and you shall be my witnesses both in Jerusalem, and in all Judea and Samaria, and even to the remotest part of the earth" (Acts 1:8). Indeed, the spread of the gospel, initiated by the apostles and continued by those they discipled, would have a broader scope than the works of the Savior during His time on earth.

To fulfill the Great Commission, believers must abide in Christ. It is impossible to fulfill the Great Commission apart from abiding . Jesus said as much: "He who abides in Me, and I in him, he bears much fruit, for apart from Me you can do nothing" (John 15:5). Notice that Jesus refers to the fruit of doing, pointing back to His statement, "greater works than these he will do" (John 14:12). Jesus then concluded, "My Father is glorified by this, that you bear much fruit, and so prove to be My disciples" (John 15:8).

Jesus concludes the theme of abiding in Christ to fulfill the Great Commission by praying for the disciples in John 17. Having already prayed for His inner circle of apostles in the Upper Room, Jesus also prayed for us: "I do not ask on behalf of these alone, but for those also who believe in Me through their word; that they may all be one; even as You, Father, are in Me and I in You, that they also may be in Us, so the world may believe that You sent Me" (John 17:20–21). Jesus prayed that the disciples would abide in Him. If they did, the world would believe He had been sent by the Father. Notice that Jesus' prayer is first of all a prayer that they would abide in Christ, "that they also may be in Us." The implication is that by abiding in Christ, they would disciple the world according to Christ's command.

The Plan's Foundation and Fulfillment

Let's take a closer look at our commission:

> And Jesus came up and spoke to them, saying, "All authority has been given to Me in heaven and on earth. Go therefore and make disci-

ples of all the nations, baptizing them in the name of the Father and the Son and the Holy Spirit, teaching them to observe all that I commanded you; and lo, I am with you always, even to the end of the age" (Matt. 28:18–20).

Plan A = 3 Everys

Plan A is the result of simple, literal obedience to the Great Commission. The plan is simple: **Every** people group can be discipled and churched, as **Every** believer-priest (you, me and every obedient believer of each new generation) is prepared to do **Every** one of three discipleship tasks. The plan got off to a running start in Acts and continued to result in multiplying disciples and churches as long as these principles remained intact.

Every Believer Is a Priest, Who Is Prepared to Do Every One of Three Tasks, to Disciple and Church Every Kind of People.

What does that mean?

The first implication is that every believer has been given full authority to obey all of Christ's commands, including the Great Commission, and has access to the Holy Spirit's leading and empowering. In other words, every believer is a priest, fully capable of full obedience. Evangelism and discipling aren't just for "professionals" like missionaries and pastors.

A second implication is that there are three essential components. The Great Commission is more than just evangelism. It also includes baptism and churching as a way for believers to obey all of Christ's commands, becoming disciples in community. All three tasks are required for healthy discipleship.

Obeying the Great Commission doesn't mean every believer will accomplish all three Great Commission tasks. Our obedience simply means that we train others in all three tasks and see each of the tasks as necessarily connected. All believers should share the gospel. And some will succeed in reaching, baptizing and training those who respond to obey, including starting new churches. Many other believers share the gospel faithfully but realize with time that their primary areas of giftedness are not in evangelism and training new believers. These people continue to share the gospel and complete the body of Christ by fulfilling other vital roles.

The third implication is that Christ desires for people from every ethnic group, in every place, to know Him and be discipled. Every individual should have this opportunity. That will only happen when we totally obey the Great Commission.

Some might concede defeat by saying, "Not every believer will do it." True, not every believer will obey the Great Commission in its entirety. But every believer should understand it, share the gospel and feel its burden; they should know that we are all responsible for obeying the Great Commission. If they choose to ignore it, they're missing out on a greater experience of Christ's power and presence.

We might exclaim, "But we don't do it that way anymore!" Indeed, we usually don't, but what would happen if we did? We could expect to see a Great Commission re-en-ACT-ment. We would see more people professing faith in Christ, being baptized, gathering in multiplying churches in all ethnic groups. Christ's presence and power would be evident—and true believers would become fully mature disciples of Christ.

2. What's Missing in Our Great Come-Mission?

Before looking in depth at how to implement *Plan A*, it's necessary to provide some biblical background.

God's missionary heart didn't originate with the Great Commission. The Old Testament clearly demonstrates His heart for all nations. However, beginning with the apostles' ministry after Pentecost, Jesus introduced a different kind of plan, the final plan, to disciple and church the whole world. Whereas the Old Testament primarily presents a "Come-Mission," Jesus laid out a "Go-Mission." The temple's era of "come and see" has given way to the church's era of "go and tell."

The Old Testament "Come-Mission"

In the Old Testament, God told His chosen people to worship in the Jerusalem temple as the center of God's worldwide salvation strategy. The temple was considered to be the place where God was present. The Ark of the Covenant, which resided in the Temple, symbolized this reality.

God's desire was for Israel to become a light to the nations in order for the entire world to come and join God's chosen people. This was God's plan for fulfilling the Abrahamic Covenant: "And in you all of the families of the earth will be blessed" (Gen. 12:3).

God intended Israel to be His mission magnet, drawing people from all over the world. The stated purpose of Jerusalem's temple was to draw both Israelites and foreigners there to worship God. Notice what Solomon prayed as he dedicated the temple:

> Also concerning the foreigner who is not of Your people Israel, when he comes from a far country for Your name's sake (for they will hear of Your great name and Your mighty hand, and of Your outstretched arm); when he comes and prays toward this house, hear in heaven Your dwelling place, and do according to all for which the foreigner calls to You, in order that all the peoples of the earth may know Your name, to fear You, as do Your people Israel, and that they may know that this house which I have built is called by Your name (1 Kings 8:41–43).

Solomon then asked the Lord to meet the daily needs of Israel as a testimony to the world:

> … so that all the peoples of the earth may know that the LORD is God; there is no one else. Let Your heart therefore be wholly devoted to the LORD our God, to walk in His statutes and to keep His commandments, as at this day (1 Kings 8:60–61).

Although the usual pattern of Old Testament evangelism was "come," a primary exception was Jonah. God sent Jonah to the pagan Ninevites, calling for them to repent, escape God's judgment and worship the true God (Jonah 3:1-10). Except for Jonah's reluctance to obey, and his lack of joy when the people received the good news, the post-Pentecost pattern more closely resembles this model than the common "Come-Mission" pattern.

Perhaps without considering the issue, many churches and sending agencies still use an Old Testament evangelism strategy. Evangelism attempts in most churches aim at bolstering the quality and excitement of worship gatherings or other events—all with the goal of drawing people to attend. Church members are urged and reminded to invite others to these events. The idea is that once non-members attend an event at the central church campus, they'll hear the gospel and receive Christ—or at least feel compelled to attend again. Mission sending agencies attempt similar strategies when they plant Western-style churches or use platforms to draw people in order to share the gospel with them. Even when we go, it appears we're sometimes still saying, "Come!"

By themselves, these kinds of "come and see" strategies are unlikely to fulfill the Great Commission. Why? Because the Great Commission envisions believers thrust into the world by their churches to share the gospel with the lost, resulting in new local churches among all peoples. What's more, discipleship without equipping and commissioning creates a passive, and often dependent, spiritual framework for believers, especially newer ones.

"Go" strategies, on the other hand, raise the bar for Christians. This perspective takes the Great Commission seriously and seeks to equip all believers, encouraging them toward obedience and maturity in Christ.

For example, consider how God worked through Pentecost in Acts 2. Luke, the author of Acts, is clear in noting that the Jews present were from "every nation under heaven" (2:5). God uses a Babel-reversing miracle (2:6ff) to communicate the gospel to everyone, and to eventually launch the new believers back to their respective regions, where they would presumably be instrumental in the planting of churches.

To be sure, "come" approaches are often helpful for local church growth. Once a church is planted, new local believers will naturally become members. But the primary purpose of *Plan A* isn't church growth or reforming already-established churches. Rather, the primary purpose is encouraging churches to train believers to obey the Great Commission, by equipping them to reach peoples who would otherwise have no access to the gospel, or gospel communities. "Go" approaches are needed both to reach beyond our local communities and to intentionally reach *across cultural barriers*, such as ethnic differences or different languages, to disciple peoples who have no churches among them.

The New Testament Great "Go-Mission"

The Old Testament plan drew people from the outside-in. The Great Commission sends people out toward the ends of the earth.

In the Book of Acts, which covers the thirty years immediately following the ascension, we see Jesus' Great Commission spiral forcefully from Jerusalem to the ends of the earth. Luke records that the apostles' accusers shouted, "… these men who have caused trouble all over the world, …" (Acts 17:6). The death of Christianity's founder didn't end the gospel's spread. Instead, just as Gamaliel predicted, the movement couldn't be overcome because it was from God (Acts 5:38–39). Empowered by the Spirit and ordered by the Savior's plan, the word of the gospel couldn't be stopped as it exploded outward to the ends of the earth.

We must remember: the Great Commission is founded upon a completed work. Christ has died as our great sacrifice. He's risen from the dead. He indwells us with His Spirit. In the New Testament age, the priests don't stay in the temple—we are the temple (1 Cor. 6:19; Eph. 2:19–22).

What would our discipleship be like if every new believer was taught these truths?

Plan A is Undated, Not Outdated

Plan A seeks to emulate the post-Pentecost mission strategy of Acts. It's derived from what Jesus expected His disciples to do once His Spirit came upon them—and how they actually did it.

Of course, modern Christians and churches have advantages our first-century counterparts lacked. Improved transportation puts gospel messengers amid their target people groups in a matter of hours, rather than months or years. Smart phones, the Internet and social media make it possible for the gospel to travel rapidly across the globe. Mass media makes it possible to communicate to multitudes of people simultaneously.

Modern advantages should be used to facilitate the tenets of the plan, not replace it. Understanding the original Great Commission calls us back to Christ's radical plan, which is undated, not outdated. It doesn't need to be updated; it simply needs to be applied.

Generational Disciples Start Generational Churches

Here is an example of how God has built upon one man's obedience to the Great Commission. Alex was thirsty for spiritual truth. He'd begun to understand the gospel through reading a Bible. Then someone introduced him to Zack, a follower of Christ. Zack shared the gospel with Alex, who believed and was baptized.

Zack then inspired Alex to reach out to his family and friends. That same evening, Alex shared the gospel with his friend Trey. Trey believed and was baptized. With Zack's encouragement, Alex and Trey started groups that quickly became churches. To guide these groups in becoming strong biblical churches, Zack continued to disciple Alex and Trey, as well as other key believers whom God raised up from among the new congregations.

To continue, among those reached by Trey was Charlie. Charlie started a church in his home and repeated the pattern with Dustin. Generational churches continue to multiply in dramatic ways through Alex's obedience.

3. Understanding the *Plan A* Orders

After Pentecost, the disciples surely wouldn't sit tight and keep quiet about Christ's sacrifice and resurrection. So, Jesus made sure they clearly understood the plan He expected them to fulfill. Jesus was taken up into heaven only "after He had by the Holy Spirit given orders to the apostles whom He had chosen" (Acts 1:2). He gave these orders as He appeared to His apostles over a 40-day period, "speaking of things pertaining to the kingdom of God" (Acts 1:3).

Jesus imparted the Great Commission in at least five of His post-resurrection appearances. Each time he emphasized important facets of how to implement the process as given in Matthew 28:18-20. The last of these is recorded in Acts 1:8.

Having already taught His disciples the Great Commission, Christ reminded them of their empowerment for the task. He ordered them to wait in Jerusalem for the coming of the Holy Spirit (Acts 1:4). To fulfill the Great Commission, the disciples must do two things. First, live by the Spirit (abide in Christ). Second, obey the plan.

The Book of Acts describes how the apostles and the first-century church, led by the Spirit, obeyed Christ's prescribed discipleship plan. Luke gives us a picture of how, over the course of thirty years, the gospel went from Jerusalem and Judea to Samaria and the uttermost parts of the world. The early disciples didn't find it complicated to understand and implement the Great Commission.

1, 2, 3 Obey the Great Commission

One Every People Group Command: "Disciple all the Ethnic Groups."
Two Assurances of Every Believer's Priesthood:
- Christ's Authority was Given to the Disciples.
- Christ's Presence was with the Disciples.

Three Tasks for Every Believer-Priest:
- Going: "Proclaiming the Gospel to Everyone"
- Baptizing: "Immersing in Accord with the Great Commission"
- Teaching: "Training to Obey All of Christ's Commands" (beginning with the Great Commission).

The Original Great Commission Process

One Core Command

There's one core command in the Great Commission: "Make disciples of all the nations" (Matt. 28:19b). Literally translated, this core command is, "Disciple all of the ethnic groups."

Two Assurances

We're also given two assurances regarding why this plan will be fulfilled:

First, every believer has authority to do it: "All authority has been given to Me in heaven and on earth. Go therefore and make disciples of all the nations" (Matt. 28:18, 19).

Second, Christ's presence, by the indwelling Holy Spirit, accompanies each believer as we do the Great Commission: "I am with you always, even to the end of the age" (Matt. 28:20).

Three Tasks

There are three tasks for fulfilling the core command of the plan: going, baptizing and teaching:

1. "Going" implies proclaiming the gospel to everyone (Mark 16:15; Luke 24:47–48; John 20:21–23; Acts 1:8).

2. "Baptizing" tells us what to do when someone believes the gospel we've proclaimed.

3. "Training" describes what we do after someone believes and is baptized. Jesus is clear that obedience doesn't stop with baptism; obedience grows as new believers are discipled "to observe all that I commanded you" (Matt. 28:20).

As mentioned earlier, most Christians won't do all three of the tasks themselves. They should, however, realize that each task is necessary for obedience. If someone professes faith after hearing the gospel, they should be baptized. If someone is baptized, we must be committed to discipling them, so they will obey all that Jesus has commanded them. This process will take time, but it is not optional.

The goal is to teach new believers to obey the Great Commission, so that when they reach people in other places, or who aren't being reached because of ethnic and cultural differences, those people will also be trained to "go home" and obey the Great Commission. Overtime, this is how new churches can develop among each ethnic, or people, group. This is the conclusion the Great Commission is moving toward.

The following chapters are devoted to explaining these obvious, but often neglected, features of *Plan A*.

Part Two: 1, 2, 3 Go Mission!

4. One "Every Ethnic Group" Command

Disciple Every Ethnic Group

"Go therefore and make disciples of all the nations" (Matt. 28:19).

Only one actual command is recorded in the Great Commission: "Make disciples of all the ethnic groups" (*matheusate panta ta ethne* in the Greek). The other phrases in the Great Commission instruct the recipient how to accomplish this core command.

What does it mean to disciple an ethnic group?

First, it means that everyone in the ethnic group would hear the gospel and have a chance to respond. God desires for all people to come to the knowledge of the truth and be saved (1 Tim. 2:4, etc.) which means they had a chance to respond to the gospel.

Second, those who respond to the gospel would be discipled in local churches, as occurred throughout Acts. The Great Commission plan equips new believers to reach others, so they can be the local church together.

The Great Commission explains that Christ died for all the world's ethnic groups. We have no way to know exactly how Jesus would have defined an ethnic group. However, a working definition of "ethnic group" from the International Mission Board (IMB) of the Southern Baptist Convention (SBC) is "an ethnolinguistic group with a common self-identity that is shared by the various members." There are two important features to consider: ethno and linguistic. In other words, language is a primary and dominant identifying factor of a people group.

Recent data from the International Mission Board[1] has identified 11,508 ethnic groups. Of these groups, 6,607 are considered unreached (less than 2 percent Christian). Joshua Project[2] uses slightly different statistics, identifying 17,017 people groups, 7,087 of which are unreached. And of those thousands of unreached people groups, the IMB considers approximately 1,161 to be "unengaged," which means there's no strategy underway with laborers working long-term in the local language toward planting multiplying, generational churches in that people group. But there's good news: the innumerable multitude of Revelation 7:9–10 offers a glorious picture of Christ's commission finally accomplished.

Discipling All the Kinds of People

Although ethnic groups share a common language and cultural similarities, they are composed of various kinds of people. An ethnic group is the sum of all its different kinds of people, or sub-groups. Trying to reach people only like ourselves is unacceptable. Any believer who intentionally avoids or excludes people because they are different is committing sin. There's no place for prejudice and exclusion in God's kingdom.

And yet, it's worth noting that the gospel often travels along familial and ethnic lines. That's why new believers naturally reach their family members, friends, neighbors and work associates. In addition, believers must intentionally engage those in other places and among different ethnic groups as well.

Established churches primarily reach their own people group, and only secondarily reach those who aren't like them, either culturally or otherwise. *Plan A* seeks to offer a method that will at least make it more likely to reach those who aren't like us.

---

1   2004-2014 Global Research, International Mission Board, June 1, 2015. Unengaged UPG data pertains to people groups of more than 100,000 in population.
2   http://JoshuaProject.net

Reaching and Churching Their Own Kind First

People most naturally evangelize those with whom they have something in common. The commonality might be family ties, but it can also be friendship, occupation, hobbies, or something else entirely.

In the Bible, for example, the Samaritan woman first went to tell the good news to other Samaritans: "Come, see a man who told me all the things that I have done; this is not the Christ, is it?" (John 4:29).

When Jesus reached Levi (Matthew), the next verse records that at Levi's house "many tax collectors and sinners were dining with Jesus and His disciples" (Mark 2:15). It appears Levi played a role in gathering his kind, tax collectors, to hear the good news. Perhaps Levi represented a different kind of people as well, the non-fundamentalist Jews, called "sinners," who were also there.

John 1:29–50 demonstrates how Jesus and His first disciples reached their respective people groups. John and Andrew were followers of John the Baptist (same affiliation), who introduced them to Jesus. Andrew reached Peter (same family). Phillip was reached next (same city as Peter and Andrew). Phillip reached Nathanael (friend or acquaintance).

The principle of reaching one's own kind first helps us understand why whole households believed together (Acts 16:14–15, 40; 16:31–34; 18:8, etc.). It also explains the presence in Cornelius' house of his close friends, along with his family, in Acts 10:24.

In the passage that follows, notice the tendency to reach one's own kind when the disciples scattered because of persecution. Also notice that obedient believers overcome prejudice to share the gospel among other people groups. This facilitates discipleship so that no group is excluded:

> So then those who were scattered because of the persecution that occurred in connection with Stephen made their way to Phoenicia and Cyprus and Antioch, speaking the word to no one except to Jews alone. But there were some of them, men of Cyprus and Cyrene, who came to Antioch and began speaking to the Greeks also, preaching the Lord Jesus. And the hand of the Lord was with them, and a large number who believed turned to the Lord (Acts 11:19–21).

Discipling Regionally and Ethnically

Just before His ascension, Jesus mapped out the geography the Great Commission would cover: Jerusalem, Judea, Samaria and the ends of the earth (Acts 1:8).

Those who attended the Pentecost celebration of Acts 2 were distinguished by their place of origin as well as ethnicity. Luke identifies Jews, Parthians, Medes, Elamites, Cretans, Arabs, Galileans and residents of Mesopotamia, Judea, Cappadocia, Pontus and Asia (Acts 2:5–13). Those gathered heard the gospel and then scattered to evangelize their respective ethnic groups and regions. Thus, the gospel bridged from Jews to other people groups.

Generally, when Paul entered an area, he first approached Jews and God-fearers in the synagogue. This resulted in believing Jews. At the same time, some Gentiles also came to faith and apparently began reaching those within their own people group (families, friends and acquaintances). This happened in Thessalonica, as some from the synagogue "were persuaded and joined Paul and Silas, along with a large number of the God-fearing Greeks and a number of the leading women" (Acts 17:4).

Discipling a People Group = Discipling Kinds of People

Each people group is composed of various kinds of people: young and old; male and female; lower-, middle- and upper-class. They each have different family structures, jobs and hobbies. People group according to these and other similarities, especially at first.

At first glance, this seems to complicate how we implement Jesus' "every kind of people" command. It doesn't have to. After all, as Paul says in Ephesians 2, the "dividing wall of hostility" has been torn down, so all people of all kinds are no longer strangers and aliens. Now we are "fellow citizens" and "members of the household of God" (Ephesians 2:14, 19). Furthermore, we all run across different types of people in our daily lives; so, as we're faithful to evangelize those whom God has providentially placed before us, different kinds of people will be reached with the gospel. Although we shouldn't try to push congregations to be ethnically and socially diverse, we must be faithful to disciple all kinds of people, knowing that God has promised to save people from every tongue, tribe and nation.

The Great Commission's vision is all-expansive; no people group gets left out or marginalized. "They won't come to our church" is no excuse. Churches naturally form among similar kinds of people. However, there aren't different kinds of churches because, in each location, the church is the inseparable body of Christ.

Upsizing Our Great Commission Vision

The Great Commission calls Christians to share the gospel with all people. Many approaches that depend on expensive facilities and highly trained leaders are only designed to reach a single community. Even when they "work," they often only reach people nearby, or those who are much like the already-existing church. That's a good start, but churches should also seek to reach people in different locations and with different characteristics.

In other words, to intend to only reach some people nearby who are a lot like us is to intend not to fulfill the Great Commission. The Great Commission vision sets the bar higher.

5. Two Assurances that Every Believer is a Priest

**"All authority has been given to Me in heaven and on earth. …
I am with you always, even to the end of the age" (Matt. 28:18a, 20b).**

Humanly speaking, the Great Commission is an impossible task. How could twelve men disciple all the ethnic groups? But the first and last statements of the Great Commission offer assurances that envelop the tasks of the Commission. Christ assures believers that He has all authority, then He assures them His continued presence will enable them to get the job done.

Christ's Authority

"All authority has been given to Me in heaven and on earth. Go therefore and make disciples of all the nations" (Matt. 28:18b–19a). Jesus proved His absolute authority with His resurrection from the dead. He then bestowed that authority on those sent to do His work. Jesus' apostles, and those who believed because of their witness, proclaimed the gospel and began churches in His full authority to obey the entire Great Commission.

They didn't need to seek permission from any earthly authority. Christ's authority manifested itself through the words and actions of uneducated fishermen and other ordinary men, even as they stood in the presence of governors and kings.

When ordinary believers are questioned about who gave them authority to proclaim the gospel, to baptize and to teach others to obey, they can simply respond, "Jesus."

The Authority of their Message

Jesus' words in Luke 24:44–48 affirm the core message the disciples were to proclaim about Jesus Christ:

> Now He said to them, "These are My words which I spoke to you while I was still with you, that all things which are written about me in the Law of Moses and the Prophets and the Psalms must be ful-

filled." Then He opened their minds to understand the scriptures, and
He said to them, "Thus it is written, that the Christ would suffer and
rise again from the dead the third day, and that repentance for the forgiveness of sins would be proclaimed in His name to all the nations,
beginning from Jerusalem. You are witnesses of these things."

Jesus affirmed that the whole Bible is actually pointing toward
one central person: Himself. The Law of Moses, the prophets and the
Psalms represent the three divisions of the Hebrew Bible. Jesus' death
and resurrection are revealed in each. When Christians proclaim the
gospel, they join the faithful who've boldly penned and proclaimed the
same truth. From Moses and David to Isaiah, Jeremiah and Daniel, the
Old Testament authors "pre-claimed" the gospel of Jesus Christ before
it came to pass. The Bible begins with the promised suffering Savior
(Gen. 3:15) and the New Testament ends with the return of the Word of
God, whose robe is dipped in blood (Rev. 19:13).

Furthermore, not only were first-century Christians not ashamed
to proclaim the gospel, they proclaimed it with the full authority of the
King of heaven and earth. Disciples of Jesus Christ never have to won-
der if they have what it takes to share the gospel with anyone, anywhere,
at any time. Jesus has already promised it.

The Authority of their Miracles

The gospel message was sometimes authenticated by miracles. They
affirmed that God delighted in the gospel's proclamation. The first
recorded persecution in Acts resulted from the proclamation of the
gospel after Christ healed a lame beggar. Notice the content of the
prayer as believers rejoiced over Peter and John's boldness to proclaim
the gospel to their persecutors: "Grant that Your bondservants may
speak Your word with all confidence, while You extend Your hand to
heal, and signs and wonders take place through the name of Your holy
servant Jesus" (Acts 4:29b–30). Bold proclamation is accompanied by
the display of Christ's power.

The apostles' miracles were extensions of Jesus' miracles. Even the
Jewish elders could not overlook the fact that remarkable miracles were
taking place: "For the fact that a noteworthy miracle has taken place
through them is apparent to all who live in Jerusalem, and we cannot
deny it" (Acts 4:16).

Why were miracles present? Miracles verified the authority of the gospel message. Where people were receptive, miracles helped them come to genuine faith (as in John 20:31). Peter's healing of Aeneas' paralysis resulted in all those who saw him in Lydda and Sharon turning to the Lord (Acts 9:35). When Peter raised Dorcas from the dead, people from all over Joppa believed in the Lord (Acts 9:42). In Acts, miracles of healing primarily occurred through the apostles, but not exclusively. Stephen and Phillip also performed miracles, and the powerful prayers of other believers resulted in miraculous answers, such as Peter's release from prison (Acts 12:3–12).

Further, the disciples prayed for boldness to proclaim the gospel, while healings, signs and wonders were performed in Jesus' name (Acts 4:29-30). This prayer was offered as the result of persecution that came because of the lame beggar's healing at the temple. It's clear that miracles often bring seekers to faith, even as they simultaneously harden those who reject the gospel.

We've learned to expect miracles as we abide in Christ and implement Plan A. When the gospel has entered new areas and people groups, the Lord has often accompanied the proclamation of the gospel with notable miracles. Many critically ill people, both physically and spiritually, have been healed, testifying to the gospel's authority. As in Acts, this has resulted in many others coming to faith in Christ, and also has intensified persecution by those who refuse to believe the gospel. Those through whom God has performed miracles humbly admit, "It's not about the miracle; it's about the gospel."

The definition of "miracle" varies. Also, miracles are by nature difficult to verify as they violate normal principles of nature. However as reliable testimonies accumulate, it's hard to deny that God still shows His power through answered prayer and supernatural intervention, especially in the context of discipling unreached people groups. Following are a few of many reliable accounts from a generational, multiplying church movement among Muslims.

Words can hardly describe the awe I felt as I listened to Sonny, a new believer, share his story of being healed from a chronic illness through the prayer of the believer who was witnessing to him. "Until last week my life was a wreck. My hands were continually shaking so badly that I could no longer do my job. I could barely eat, much less read a book."

Harry, himself a relatively new believer, prayed for Sonny in Jesus name and proclaimed the gospel to him. Sonny was now saved and steady as a rock. The Lord had miraculously healed him! As we worshipped together, like in Acts, no one could deny that a notable miracle had taken place.

Sonny, with his wife and three adult children, formed the first house church in a large unreached area. In response to God's grace, Sonny added, "Now I'm fasting twice weekly and preparing so I can reach others."

Jonah and his family had lost hope. His kidney disease was reaching the critical stage. Jonah was resting at his home with drainage tubes coming from his body when Joe and Sally came to visit him. They proclaimed the gospel and invited Jonah to believe. After Jonah responded in faith to the gospel, the Lord miraculously healed him. His friends were amazed, and many of them believed in Christ. Jonah joyfully returned to work a day or two later.

The doctors had given up on Sarah's recovery from a stroke that left her virtually paralyzed and unable to speak. She was deteriorating, and her family was called in to be with her in her last days. But she was visited by a husband and wife who knew the Savior had power to heal. They entered Sarah's room and shared the gospel with her. Being unable to speak, Sarah still found a way to express faith in the gospel. The couple prayed for Sarah. Afterward, she began to move. After a series of visits, Sarah's health progressed to where she now walks and proclaims the gospel to others.

Many times, God Himself prepares hearts of people to receive Him through miracles. And then He calls them, like Paul, to believe the gospel and proclaim it to others. Ahmad, a former Muslim imam, recounts his own spiritual journey as follows:

> For more than forty years, as part of the Muslim prayer ritual, I prayed five times daily, "Show me the straight way." I really meant it. After forty years of searching, one overcast evening as I stood on my porch, a light from heaven came into me. I knew that was Jesus. I told a local pastor about my experience, but he was afraid. However, he gave me a Bible and told me to read it.

Ahmad became frustrated and angry as he read the Torah, because he didn't see Jesus' name there. He decided to burn the Bible. But as he prepared to set it on fire, the Spirit told him to put his finger into the

Bible and open it there. Doing so, Ahmad opened the Bible to John 14:6 and read, "Jesus answered, 'I am the way and the truth and the life. No one comes to the Father except through Me.'"

The rest is history.

Christ's Accompaniment

"I am with you always, even to the end of the world" (Matt. 28:20b).

In the Upper Room, Jesus promised, "I will not leave you as orphans; I will come to you" (John 14:18). Further, He concluded His High Priestly prayer with the affirmation, "I in them" (John 17:26). Indeed, it was in the same Upper Room where, 50 days after His resurrection, Jesus came to the disciples through the Holy Spirit. As the disciples obeyed the Great Commission, they were never alone. Christ abided in them as they abided in Him.

Jesus, through the Holy Spirit, indwells every believer. First Peter 2:5 also emphasizes this: "You also, as living stones, are being built up as a spiritual house for a holy priesthood, to offer up spiritual sacrifices acceptable to God through Jesus Christ." The "spiritual building" mentioned in this verse isn't a literal building. We are the building. Metaphorically speaking, we are the "temple." Practically speaking, we are the "holy priesthood." The "spiritual house" and the "holy priesthood" are two different ways of saying, "We are the Spirit-indwelled priests" (1 Cor. 6.19–20; 2 Cor. 6:16).[3]

Christ's presence with the disciples was evident as He answered their prayers, guided them through dangerous situations and gave them wisdom for each situation. He was with them, and He is with us until the end of the world.

Reading Acts, one notices the familiarity and expectation with which the early Christians prayed to the Lord. He had previously promised in the Upper Room, "If you ask Me anything in My name, I will do it" (John 14:14). The disciples took Him up on it.

As first-century disciples shared the gospel, Christ's presence (by the Spirit's filling) empowered them. On at least six occasions in Acts,

---

3   A full discussion of priesthood of the believer is laid out in Chapter 11, "We Really Are Real Priests."

the disciples were said to be filled with the Spirit.[4] Each of these occasions pertains to either speaking God's Word or preparing to do so. The filling of the Spirit is functional. The purpose of the Spirit's filling is effective service. The Holy Spirit helps Christians when they are doing the works of Christ. This isn't all the Spirit does for the Christian, but it's a significant part.

Without the Spirit's help, we can't succeed. Practically, it's the filling of the Spirit that enables believers to excel in ministry far beyond their own ability. We're not sufficient in ourselves to become ministers of the gospel, but God makes us sufficient (2 Cor. 3:4–6).

---

4   The filling of disciples with the Spirit is recounted in Acts 2:4-13; 4:8-12, 31; 6:3, 5; 7:55-56; 9:17; and 11:24.

6. Task 1: Every Believer Goes to Proclaim the Gospel

The core command of the Great Commission is fulfilled by doing three tasks. Each of these tasks is written as a participle in the original language. This doesn't lessen their importance; rather, they complement the core command by showing its parts. In that sense, these tasks can be seen as complementary to the primary command. Every believer who obeys the Great Commission proclaims the gospel and is prepared to baptize and to teach the new believer to obey the Great Commission as a basis for reaching others who will obey all of Christ's commands together.

Going = Proclaiming the Gospel to Everyone

That the apostles and first-century disciples would be going was never in doubt, as emphasized by a literal translation of Matt. 28:19a: "Going, disciple all of the ethnic groups." Everyone went. Those who didn't immediately go were often forced out by persecution. However, as they went out, they fulfilled the Great Commission as they shared the gospel with everyone in their paths.

The Good News

To go was to proclaim the gospel. Paul reminded the Corinthians of the message he proclaimed to them:

> Christ died for our sins according to the Scriptures, and that He was buried, and that He was raised on the third day according to the Scriptures, and that He appeared to Cephas, then to the twelve. After that He appeared to more than five hundred brethren at one time, most of whom remain until now, but some have fallen asleep .... (1 Cor. 15:3b–6).

The essential elements of the gospel message can be summarized by the "CORE" acronym:

C: Jesus was **C**rucified for our sins
O: **O**rdained by God (as evidenced through fulfilled Scripture)
R: **R**aised from the dead

E: confirmed by Eyewitnesses.[5]

In Acts, the gospel always included the following basic content:

1. Jesus (identified as Messiah, and often as Lord) died for the sins of those receiving the witness.

2. He was raised from the dead.

3. This was foretold in prophecies and confirmed by witnesses.

4. Responding to the gospel by repentance and faith results in forgiveness of sins.

5. Jesus is often presented as Judge and refusing to receive the gospel results in judgment.[6]

Going with the Gospel in Acts

The apostles' primary calling was as witnesses to the resurrection of Christ (Acts 1:22, 2:32, 3:15, etc.). As they lived by the Spirit, they proclaimed that Christ had died and risen again, and that those who, through repentance and faith, received the gospel would be forgiven of their sins. Those who received the gospel were expected to then proclaim it to others. New believers naturally share the gospel, especially when they're expected to.

Eager Heralds of Good News

Filter with the Gospel

The only way to know if someone is open to the gospel is to share it with them and find out. Once we began filtering with the gospel, we were amazed at how many times those we considered closed to the gospel message were ready to receive Christ and become disciples.

There are no instances in Acts where the first-century believers waited to share the gospel past the first meeting. They had an intentional strategy, and it was simple: meet people, build rapport, share the

---

5   The CORE acronym was devised by Keith McKinley as a way to summarize the gospel message.

6   These characteristics of gospel presentations in Acts were identified by Mark Stevens after he noticed similarities between witnessing in Acts and the Any-3 method. Mark observed that Any-3 combines the content of the gospel presentations of Acts with the evangelism style of Jesus in John 4.

gospel in a way they could understand it and provide an opportunity to respond. When those who heard the gospel were open, appropriate follow-up was offered with the goal of leading those persons to faith.

This strategy reflects Paul's heart, too. As he writes to the Corinthians: "For Christ did not send me to baptize, but to preach the gospel, not in cleverness of speech, so that the cross of Christ would not be made void" (1 Cor. 1:17). Paul indicates here that cleverness of speech can dilute the power of the gospel. In my book *Any-3*, I mention tactics that poison evangelism.[7] For example, when we devise approaches to "earn a right" for the gospel to be heard, they often lessen the gospel's power.

Spiritual talk isn't the same as proclaiming the gospel. In my own experience, I found that we'd often talk about Jesus, but our relationships were ending before we shared the gospel. Another error was that we'd share several spiritual truths from different angles; when we finally shared the gospel, it simply became one of many truths about Jesus, rather than the one and only truth that saves. We've learned it's best to focus on presenting the clear, simple gospel as our first objective. Then, depending on how people respond, we proceed to other spiritual truths.

No matter how creative or logical, human-derived evangelistic paradigms are often ineffective, eroding the enthusiasm of those who would otherwise be bold in evangelism. Many approaches share everything but the gospel up front. Then, once a relationship has been established, the gospel is finally shared. However, the power isn't in the prelude; the power is in the gospel itself.

The gospel is God's power (*dunamis*, Rom. 1:16), which demolishes sinners' hardened hearts, then regenerates them as the Holy Spirit convicts of sin and draws people to faith in Christ. This is how Jesus explains the Holy Spirit's work:

> And He, when He comes, will convict the world concerning sin and righteousness and judgment; concerning sin, because they do not believe in Me; and concerning righteousness, because I go to the Father and you no longer see Me; and concerning judgment, because the ruler of this world has been judged (John 16:8–11).

According to these verses, the Holy Spirit loudly, clearly and repeatedly says three things to lost people. This occurs both before and while

---

7   Mike Shipman, Any-3: Lead Muslims to Christ Now! (Monument, Colorado: WIGTake Resources, 2013), pp. 63-74.

hearing the gospel, but especially afterward. First, the Spirit says, "Not believing in Jesus is sin." Second, he says, "Jesus is righteous, but you aren't." Finally, he says, "Repent or you will be judged."

This reminds me of Manny's story. Manny was a well-educated and influential Muslim imam. During a time of economic hardship, he drove a taxi for extra cash. One day, a faithful believer shared the gospel with him in his taxi. Manny responded abruptly to the man who shared with him, but he couldn't get the gospel out of his mind. He said, "It's different when someone shares this with you personally as opposed to hearing it on the radio or other media." Manny has now come to faith and is leading many other Muslims to faith, training them to start house churches. To the brother who shared with him, Manny says, "Thank you!"

Anyone, Anywhere, Anytime Evangelism

Having tried complicated, lengthy methods of presenting the gospel to Muslims, we began training believers to determine who was open or closed to the gospel by actually sharing the gospel with them.

Our desperation to see people respond to the gospel led us to develop the *Any-3* evangelism approach. We based this approach on the general framework with which Jesus evangelized the woman of Samaria (John 4:1-42), which mirrors the pattern of Acts. In short, we should be ready to share with anyone, anywhere, anytime.

In this approach, we've identified five characteristics and five steps. The characteristics of *Any-3* are simple: 1) be intentional, 2) be informal, 3) be interactive, 4) take initiative and 5) introduce the Messiah by proclaiming the gospel. The five steps are: 1) get connected, 2) get to a "God conversation," 3) get to lostness, 4) get to the gospel and 5) get to a decision.

Acts/Any-3 Method Parallels[8]

The core elements used to communicate the gospel in Acts follow a similar pattern. Generally, there was some sort of connection, followed by a discussion of sin and its results. Next, Jesus' life and works were dis-

---

8   These characteristics of witnessing in Acts were identified by Mark Stevens before he encountered Any-3. He noticed the similarities and then made the comparison.

cussed, especially His death and resurrection. Then Jesus was presented as Lord and/or Christ and Judge. These truths having been confirmed by the prophets and others, the only proper response—repentance and faith—resulted in the forgiveness of sin. In Acts, there was an urgent invitation for recipients to respond to the gospel message.

Every-Person Evangelism

Every believer should be ready to simply and relationally share the gospel with anyone, anywhere, at any time. Intentional evangelism glorifies Christ's sacrifice, allowing lost people to hear the gospel and have an opportunity to surrender themselves to Christ. Imagine the impact if every believer, including all new believers, was sharing the gospel, and more lost people were hearing the gospel and being invited to follow Jesus!

Most Christians don't share the gospel with an invitation to follow Jesus. However, when they're trained to do so and held accountable, many Christians are delighted to do what they've known they should be doing all along. This is why, immediately after new believers are brought to faith with a simple, reproducible gospel presentation and invitation, we train them in using the same presentation and invitation with their families, friends and acquaintances.

Going Here, There and Everywhere

"Going" implies believers are sharing the gospel as they go about their everyday lives. It also demands that we, like the apostles, intentionally share the gospel with all kinds of people. Not everyone will go to a distant place, but all should go to the lost with the gospel.

Evangelism in Acts occurred formally in synagogues and public gatherings, and informally among smaller groups. Paul reasoned in the synagogues, but he also witnessed every day in the marketplace in Athens with those who happened to be there (Acts 17:17). Paul's special giftedness and training gave him a platform in many forums, but he felt the need to share the gospel wherever he happened to be, just as the thousands of other believers were doubtlessly doing (Acts 8:4).

Unfortunately, most Christians today don't reproduce themselves by leading others to faith in Christ. But the Great Commission assumes that new believers will reproduce. After all, seeing lost people profess faith in Christ and join a church should be one of the highlights of the Christian life. Another highlight should be seeing those new believers in turn reach other people.

The result isn't simply more conversions, but more joy in the Lord for all Christians. As believers begin to proclaim the gospel, they're filled with the Spirit's joy and experience personal renewal. Many believers and ministry teams are being set free as they shift to an every-person evangelism paradigm. One team has adopted this slogan: "Anyone who knows me gets to hear the gospel!"[9] This team is making an impact on everyone they meet. As they're introducing the lost to Christ, many believers have made evangelism a part of their lifestyle.

Start with Individuals, Groups, or Crowds

In Acts, the gospel was shared to individuals, groups and crowds. In some passages, new churches would emerge as people responded in faith. In other passages, such as Acts 2:41–47, new believers were gathered into an existing church.

Evangelize Individuals and Train Them to do Plan A

In Acts, some individuals heard the gospel, believed and began proclaiming the good news. As the primary example, Paul immediately began to proclaim Jesus to others (Acts 9:20). Similarly, the Ethiopian eunuch, according to church history, planted the church in Ethiopia. Another example would be the Philippian jailer who called out, "What must I do to be saved" (Acts 16:30)? Having believed the gospel, he gathered his whole household to hear it as well, resulting in reaching them all. The goal is never to reach only an individual. When individuals come to faith, an immediate objective is to equip them to reach others, forming churches.

Evangelize a Group and Train Those Who Believe to do Plan A

Often in Acts, a group of people heard the gospel simultaneously. For instance, Paul usually began his ministry in a city by proclaiming the gospel in the synagogue. In other instances, the gospel was proclaimed in less formal settings. In these situations, the aim was to proclaim the

---

9   This approach is exemplified by JT, who leads this team.

gospel to the group in order to find those who were open. Those who responded then proclaimed the gospel to their own families and acquaintances. Together, all who believed formed a church. Several times, whole families came to faith this way, such as the families of Lydia and the Philippian jailer in Acts 16:14–40.[10]

Note that the groups who came to faith together were initially gathered by a group member who had already heard the gospel, not by the outsider who proclaimed it. The one exception to this, Cornelius, had a supernatural visitation that prepared him to send for a gospel messenger, having not yet heard the gospel himself. On this occasion, the entire group believed the gospel (Acts 10:34–48).

Evangelize a Crowd and Train Those Who Believe to do Plan A

Sometimes, the gospel was proclaimed to a larger crowd (Acts 2:14–36; 3:11–26; 8:1–12; 17:22-34). Those who believed came together to become churches, or perhaps joined existing churches. Many of them joined the effort to implement the Great Commission in other areas.

In conclusion, evangelism in Acts took place individually as well as with groups and crowds. Each time, the goal was to lead those open to the gospel to faith, then send them out to reach their families, friends and others. The rapid and thorough expansion of the church from Jerusalem to Rome indicates that new believers understood they were expected to share the gospel—and many did.

Getting Ready to Go

It's preferable to have a simple, transferrable method for sharing the gospel. That way, new believers can learn more easily how to share with others. Of course, the Spirit might lead you to a different gospel-sharing method, but He will never lead you to a different gospel message.

Just this week, some friends and I were touring near a large city where gospel access is restricted. One night we were walking around town praying for opportunities to share the gospel with those whom God was preparing. A pair of my friends met a man who was reading a

---

10   In the case of Lydia, there was a place of prayer rather than a synagogue. There are no indications in Acts that any entire synagogue congregation came to faith and formed a church.

book about hell. My friends shared the gospel with him. He professed faith in Christ and was baptized the next day. The Holy Spirit had quite obviously convicted this man of judgment, so his heart was prepared to hear the gospel. My friends were simultaneously prepared to share the gospel. This man is already proclaiming the gospel to his family members and friends!

7. Task 2: Every Believer Prepared to Baptize Those They Lead to Christ

Baptizing in the Great Commission

Jesus commanded His disciples to immerse new believers (*baptizontes*). Throughout the Roman Empire, when those who spoke the Greek language either read or heard Christ's baptismal command, they heard, "Immerse them." Because the Greek word was transliterated (baptize) instead of translated (immerse), modern readers often hear something different than what Jesus actually commanded.

New believers from all recognized denominations of the early church were immersed in obedience to Christ's command to identify with His death and resurrection. Only after the year 1300 A.D. was a mode other than immersion (pouring) formally recognized as an acceptable mode of baptism.[11]

Is the mode of baptism vital? I'm more convinced than ever of its importance. Baptism isn't a negotiable symbol. Rather, it's a preeminent, Christ-commanded picture of the gospel. Baptism by immersion identifies the believer with the sacrificial atonement and resurrection of Christ, reminds the church of this reality and testifies to the world about the death, burial and resurrection of Christ. Immersion is the only mode of baptism that strictly does what Jesus commanded, because it's the only one that clearly communicates the gospel.

The Acts Baptismal Pattern

Based on the authority given by Christ in the Great Commission, *all* believers have the authority to baptize new believers in the name of the Father, Son, and Holy Spirit. Therefore, everyone who believes the gospel can immediately profess their new faith by being baptized.

---

11   Harold Clapper, "A Short History of Immersion," CharlesDailey.net/baptism.html

The following passages in Acts model or discuss baptism: 2:37–41; 8:4–13, 8:36–38; 9:10–19; 10:47–48; 16:13–15, 27–34; 18:5–8; 19:1–5; and 22:14–16.

When studying these passages, ask these questions:

1. Who was baptized?

2. What happened prior to their baptism to bring them to faith?

3. When were they baptized in relation to their profession of faith?

4. How were they baptized?

5. Who baptized them?

Reviewing these biblical baptismal examples will reveal what changes need to be made to our current baptismal practices.

In Acts, the baptismal pattern can be described with this acrostic: A, E, I, O, U: **A**fter profession of faith, **E**veryone is **I**mmersed by the **O**ne who won or witnessed their profession, with **U**rgency.

After their profession of faith, new believers were baptized. This is clearly the teaching of Jesus. Pre-conversion baptism is never described in the New Testament. Two of three instances in Acts where an entire family was baptized report that the person and his household believed before being baptized.

Every new believer who professed faith was expected to be baptized. Specific baptisms are mentioned ten times in Acts. These instances affirm the baptismal pattern and the assumption that even when baptism isn't mentioned, new believers were baptized according to this pattern.

Immersion was the exclusive mode of baptism in Acts. When the mode is indicated, new believers come up out of the water. Immersion symbolizes with the actual bodies of new believers that they have expressed faith in the death, burial and resurrection of Christ. Baptism by immersion illustrates the gospel.

Either the **O**ne who reached a new believer baptized them, or the baptism was performed by someone else who was present at the time of the new believer's profession of faith. There are no examples in Acts of an outsider being brought in to baptize a new believer whom another person had reached. Also, there are no explicit examples of the new believer being brought to an outsider for baptism. This might be surprising, especially when we consider the weight many denominations put on the exclusivity of baptism by an ordained leader. Acts rarely says who baptized new converts. Though Philip immersed the Ethiopian eunuch and Ananias immersed Paul, in most cases we simply don't know.

Practically speaking, it would have been not just improbable, but impossible for the Twelve, or people they appointed, to baptize every new convert. The best explanation for how people were baptized as the gospel traveled from Jerusalem to the ends of the earth is that, based on the authority of the Great Commission, people were baptized by those who reached them.

Baptism by the person who reached the new convert sets up a natural mentoring relationship. However, when the new believer is given to a third party for baptism, the mentor-mentee relationship is more easily broken. This also breaks the Great Commission pattern for the new believer to go, baptize and train others to do the same.

One day, Jarrod woke up late for his college class. In a hurry, he quickly put on a jacket without a shirt. His roommate urged him to at least wear a shirt, so he hurriedly put on a white T-shirt under the jacket and rushed off to class. Afterward, he was driving home on his motorcycle when a thunderstorm forced him to stop under an overhang at the home of a stranger, a Muslim man named Abu.

Jarrod already evangelized regularly and took this opportunity to share the gospel. Abu leaned forward and listened very intently. When invited to surrender to Jesus, Abu responded and was baptized. Afterward, Abu explained to Jarrod that he had experienced three dreams about Jesus. In the first dream, Jesus was dressed in white and was so bright that Abu had to cover his eyes. In the second, Jesus told Abu to come to Him, but Abu was afraid and ran away. The third dream occurred the night before Jarrod came. Jesus told Abu that a man in a white shirt would arrive the next day to explain the intent of the dreams to him.[12] Since that time, Jarrod's preparedness to obey the entire Great Commission has given him the opportunity to plant many multiplying churches, not merely groups of unbaptized believers.

Urgency of baptism means that baptism was immediate. In fact, there are no examples of new believers waiting before they were baptized. Paul's baptism, although occurring three days after the vision on the road to Damascus, fits this pattern as well. In that situation, Paul

---

12   This story was shared with the author by Dr. Trevor Castor.

was baptized as soon as Ananias came to him three days after the vision and explained the implications of receiving the gospel. Ananias said to him, "Now why do you delay? Get up and be baptized, and wash away your sins, calling on His name" (Acts 22:16).

Baptism was never optional or intentionally delayed for those who professed faith; baptism *was* their profession of faith.[13]

Baptism = Immersion into the Body of Christ

When one is baptized into Christ, he or she is simultaneously baptized into the body of Christ. This often means the new believer joins an existing church. But in frontier mission situations, as was often the case in Acts, the new believer might be the first member of a new church[14]— one that they, Lord willing, will someday gather as others around them come to faith.

Even if no one else has come to faith, in situations like this, if possible, the new believer will continue to meet regularly with those who led them to faith, enfolding into their church as well as they can. Simultaneously, they're sharing the gospel with friends, relatives and acquaintances—with the hopes of starting a new church.[15] For most new believers in frontier contexts, one of the best things that can happen is for them to reach others, forming a new local church.

---

13   In general, those who are being baptized by outsiders in Plan A movements are adults (usually heads of households). Almost always, the children who are coming to faith and being baptized are those whose parent(s) have professed faith.

14   "Church" of course refers to baptized believers who have covenanted together and function as a biblical church (see Chapter 13). Since the church is a gathering of believers, instead of a place, it really doesn't matter where "house churches" meet. They may meet anywhere Christ's followers can gather together and function as churches.

15   This is perhaps the best way to explain the concept. However, the reality on the field is much more fluid. Discipleship and mentoring also happening day by day, life on life and in the believer's own walk with Christ. The Spirit sanctifies them using multiple predictable and unpredictable factors.

Baptismal Breakthroughs

The A, E, I, O, U pattern of baptism reflects the scriptural pattern. To plant healthy, multiplying churches, we must obey the entire Great Commission, not just two-thirds of it. This means that a believer must be prepared to go, baptize and teach new believers to obey all of Christ's commands.

Public or Private Baptism?

In Acts, baptism happened publicly and privately. The 3,000 people who believed at Pentecost (Acts 2:41) were certainly baptized publicly. Peter and some believers from Joppa attended when the Gentiles at Cornelius' house were baptized. However, it appears that only Ananias was present at Paul's baptism, while other new believers and family members were present at the baptism of the families of Cornelius, Lydia and the Philippian jailer (Acts 16). Regardless of who attended the baptismal event, there is no indication that outside parties were brought in to witness baptisms.

Baptism is a profession of faith in the gospel of Christ. Sometimes it's public, sometimes it happens only with the baptizer in attendance. The emphasis at baptism was the new believer's identification with Christ's death and resurrection, rather than its public or private nature. Certainly, genuine conversion leads to public profession, but not necessarily at the baptism event itself.

8. Task 3: Every Believer Taught to Obey All of Christ's Commands

Teaching: Training New Disciples to Obey All of Jesus' Commands, while Immediately Obeying the Great Commission Command

The third task that must be done is "teaching them to observe all that I commanded you" (Matt. 28:20a).

Jesus designed the Great Commission so that believers and churches would multiply, so that every kind of people would be reached with the gospel and churched.

Train Them to Obey Christ's First Commands

First, it should be noted that "teaching them to observe" entails transferred knowledge and skills, resulting in obedience. The result is that new believers obey the commands, not just understand what they are.

Second, note that although the Great Commission was given specifically to the Twelve Apostles, they were to teach those they reached to obey this and all other commands as well. Therefore, the commands of Christ for the Twelve were given to all believers to obey.

Those who fulfill the Great Commission teach new converts to obey the Great Commission. It's vital in unreached areas for new believers to know this so they and other new believers can obey Christ's commands together and stand together as the body of Christ when opposition arises.

The task of teaching others sounds intimidating, especially for a new believer. How can they teach, when they themselves are new in the faith? They can teach others to do the simple things that were modeled for them: sharing the gospel, reading the Bible, praying. They can also help new believers understand a simple pattern for studying the Scripture, both together and as individuals. More than anything else, the new believer must be confident that the Holy Spirit uses both Scripture and other believers to continue the training process. As they themselves learn, they're growing in their own ability to disciple others.

Discipleship includes spiritual disciplines, character development and basic skills. We don't delay training disciples how to study the Bible, pray and worship. In fact, in most cases we've modeled each of these critical components from the beginning of the follow-up and discipleship process. In the following list of early training objectives, notice that in each step, the witness has already modeled the task with the new believer as a basis for training. What we do for the new believer, the new believer will then do for those he or she leads to faith.

It's worth noting as well that we don't delay any topic the new convert needs to learn. Life-on-life teaching is essential to help new believers face real life struggles. However, we immediately begin training new believers to obey the Great Commission. As they grow in grace in the knowledge of the Savior, the best thing we can do for them is train them to reach others, forming churches where together they can become mature disciples.

Early Great Commission Training Objectives

First, train new believers to lead others to faith, using the same pattern you modeled when you led them to faith.

Second, train them to follow up with those interested in the gospel, the same way a field-worker should have followed with them.

Third, train them to baptize those who profess faith in Christ, using the same pattern you modeled for them when you baptized them.

Fourth, train them to gather and facilitate a simple, interactive church meeting, the way you modeled when you began discipling them.

Fifth, train them to train new believers to repeat the process with each new believer they lead to faith.

There's More Than Rapid Multiplication!

Four imperatives of Plan A set DNA for healthy church and leadership development. First, lead with gospel proclamation. Second, teach new believers from unreached places and peoples to gather those who are open to the gospel to study God's word. Third, set a clear path for groups to become biblical churches. Fourth, implement a primarily indigenous leadership training pattern that emphasizes both multiplication and deeper spiritual growth (going and growing).

We should long for, in fact pray for, the rapid spread of the gospel in each area, resulting in church formation. However, church and leadership development take time. Extensive teaching and appropriate assisting are essential. As groups and churches form, they need guidance to become mature churches that obey Scripture. Also, ongoing leadership training must be implemented so that group leaders grow in their relationship with Christ and develop the knowledge and skills necessary to lead churches.

How many of Christ's commands should new believers obey? All of them. Paul stated his apostolic vision was to:

> [Be] a minister of Christ Jesus to the Gentiles, ministering as a priest the gospel of God, so that my offering of the Gentiles may become acceptable, sanctified by the Holy Spirit. Therefore in Christ Jesus, I will not presume to speak of anything except what Christ has accomplished through me, resulting in the obedience of the Gentiles by word and deed (Rom. 15:16–18).

The ultimate goal of *Plan A* is to offer to God full obedience by word and deed of every kind of people. The ultimate goal is complete discipleship, both quantitatively and qualitatively.[16]

Train Them to Obey All of Christ's Commands

Christ unequivocally stated the foremost commandments of God:

Jesus answered, "Hear, O Israel! The Lord our God is one Lord; and you shall love the Lord your God with all your heart, and with all your soul, and with all your mind, and with all your strength." The second is this, "You shall love your neighbor as yourself." There is no other commandment greater than these (Mark 12:29–30).

These two commandments form the basis for all of Christ's commandments, and obeying the Great Commission is foundational for obeying these commandments. New believers begin knowing God as a foundation for loving Him and form a church to grow in their love for God and one another.

Once believers are obeying Christ's initial commands (repenting and believing the gospel, being baptized, proclaiming the gospel to others, worshiping together as Christ's church and training others to do the

---

16   See also Colossians 1:28-29, which restates Paul's desire to present every man complete in Christ.

same), they will pursue obedience to all His commands. This happens further as church leaders are trained to facilitate the spiritual growth of those they shepherd (Eph. 4:11–12).

Churches not only desire that every person hears the gospel; they also desire to bring every believer to full maturity in Christ. As Paul said, "We proclaim Him, admonishing every man and teaching every man with all wisdom, so that we may present every man complete in Christ" (Col. 1:28).

For all, that will include evangelizing their friends and neighbors; for some, that will include planting churches in unreached places and among unreached peoples.

Part Three:
It Happened Once; It's Happening Again

9. Telescopic Glasses to See the Original Plan in Action

Because of our experience, we usually understand the Great Commission through the lens of contemporary methods and evangelistic strategies. But what would happen if we saw clearly how the Great Commission was fulfilled in the first century? What if we were to implement the same pattern today?

Acts shows how the Great Commission was fulfilled in the first thirty years after Christ's ascension. Discipleship and church planting exploded from Jerusalem to Rome. The result was a living, growing church that looked drastically different from what we often see today.

The majesty of the Great Commission is its profound simplicity. God Himself personally intervenes to guarantee that the commission succeeds. So ultimately, it's not the "plan" that works; it's the Spirit Who makes the Great Commission work, just as He did in Acts.

Plan A in and from the Upper Room

The gospel of John was written near the end of the first century, recounting how Christ had foretold the fulfillment of the Great Commission. Although the apostles might not have fully understood all Jesus was saying in the Upper Room at the time, in retrospect it was crystal clear. The theme of the Upper Room discourse, as recorded by John, is simple: Glorify God by abiding in Christ, to fulfill the Great Commission.

The Upper Room Discourse of John 13-17 serves as a preparation manual for Christ's original disciples, and for modern disciples who desire to see the Great Commission fulfilled. Immersing oneself in this crucial teaching by Jesus is perhaps the best way to prepare to experience His greater works, the discipleship movement of Acts.

We'll see later that the church-planting pattern of Acts follows the ABIDES acrostic.[17] Looking back, we notice this pattern in the Upper Room Discourse as well.

Foretold in the Upper Room, Fulfilled in Acts

Abide in Christ (Live in the Spirit)

In the Upper Room, Jesus commanded His disciples to "Abide in Me" (John 15:4a). As they abided in Christ, they would glorify God by bearing much fruit (John 15:7–8). The world would know that God sent Jesus if they were abiding in Him (John 17:20–23).

The correlation between abiding in Christ and fruit-bearing is obvious. However, it's not formulaic. For instance, Jesus didn't imply that, "the number of souls a person will win is proportionate to the extent of his abiding in Christ." Often, Great Commission fruit is hidden to us, while obvious to God. Seeing abiding in Christ as directly proportionate to numerical results would foster either pride among the "successful" or shame among those who didn't produce obvious numerical results.

---

17   The ABIDES acrostic was originally "ABIDE." The "S" was added as a reminder to repeat the process. "ABIDE" communicates concepts similar to those of 1) "ARROW," developed by the Southern Baptist Convention's International Mission Board's Southeast Asia leadership team, and 2) "Four Fields," developed by Nathan Shank and further refined by Neill Mims and Steve Smith.

Abiding in Christ is the same reality as living in the Spirit. Jesus promised He would indwell His disciples (John 14:20). That promise was fulfilled at Pentecost. In Acts, the proof that the disciples were abiding in Christ was living in the Holy Spirit—the Spirit of Jesus Christ (as in Acts 16:7). To abide in Christ is to live in the Holy Spirit.

Boldly Proclaim the Gospel

Jesus had foretold that the apostles would be His witnesses: "He [the Spirit] will testify about Me, and you will testify also, because you have been with Me from the beginning" (John 15:26–27). Beginning in Jerusalem and advancing to the ends of the earth, the apostles and those they reached proclaimed that Christ had been both crucified for the forgiveness of sins and raised from the dead. If people would believe this message through repentance and faith, their sins would be forgiven.

Instill Multiplication in New Believers while Discipling Them

The disciples who abided in Christ could expect multiplying, lasting fruit (John 15:1–8, 16). This occurred in Acts as new believers shared the gospel and gathered their families and friends to become disciples together.

Develop Churches Through the New Believers Who Multiply

The concept of churching is fully developed in Acts, but one notices that the functions of church were mentioned in the Upper Room as well. Jesus foretold what His disciples would do together. They would be sanctified by His truth (discipleship), see His glory and know that God sent Jesus (worship, including prayer as in John 16:23-27, etc.), abide in Christ together (fellowship), love one another (ministry) and witness (evangelism). In other words, they would become the church.[18]

Equip Leaders in a Reproducible Way

Among Jesus' primary works was to equip His disciples. Before His earthly departure, He finished this equipping, commending them to God (John 17:4–12). Equipping churches and their leaders became a

---

18   These church functions were implied and described by Jesus in His high priestly prayer (John 17).

primary emphasis in Acts as well. The work of the Spirit. and ongoing contacts through visits and letters, insured that discipleship would continue in areas where churches were forming.

Send Believers to New Areas and Peoples

Jesus prepared His disciples, then sent them to do His work. He prayed that those they led to Christ would do the same, so that the world would know that God sent Jesus out of love (John 17:20–23). Jesus envisioned generational, multiplying discipleship in which every believer would abide in Christ and disciple others. Notice that in His prayer, He had the same expectations for generational disciples as He did for the original disciples.

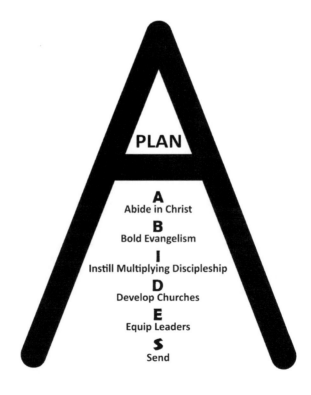

Plan A in Jerusalem, All Judea and Samaria

In Jerusalem and All Judea

The plan progressed in Jerusalem as follows: The apostles proclaimed the "mighty deeds of God," followed by Peter's presentation of the gospel and baptism for those who professed faith (Acts 2:5–41).[19] New believers multiplied as they were being added daily (Acts 2:41). They met together in homes (Acts 2:41–47) where they became mature disciples together. In addition, local believers and church leaders received ongoing discipleship and training from the apostles and other mature believers who served as leaders. From Jerusalem, believers were sent by God throughout the world as they returned home after Pentecost, were scattered because of persecution, or intentionally left to implement the Great Commission in other areas.

In Samaria and Beyond

> And on that day a great persecution began against the church in Jerusalem, and they were all scattered throughout the regions of Judea and Samaria, except the apostles. Therefore, those who had been scattered went about preaching the word. Phillip went down to the city of Samaria and began proclaiming Christ to them (Acts 8:1, 4–5).

As persecution intensified in Jerusalem, believers scattered and proclaimed the gospel wherever they went. Included in that group was Phillip, who obeyed the Spirit by going to Samaria to proclaim the gospel. Many of the Samaritans believed the gospel and were baptized (Acts 8:12,16). The number of believers multiplied as Phillip and others witnessed in all Samaria (as promised in Acts 1:8). The formation of churches isn't recorded in Acts 8, but it's reasonable to believe that it happened.

An angel directed Phillip to an encounter with an Ethiopian eunuch who was searching spiritually. After he proclaimed the gospel and baptized the Ethiopian, Phillip was called by the Spirit to Azotus, where he continued proclaiming the gospel in the villages. As for the new believer, he was filled with joy. The Bible is silent about what happened to

---

19   The biblical text doesn't say who baptized the 3,000 believers at Pentecost or where they were baptized, only that they were baptized.

the eunuch after his conversion. However, historical accounts state that he went back to Ethiopia and planted Christ's church there.

In Caesarea

Peter's divinely guided trip to Caesarea represents the first extensively recorded example of the gospel going to the Gentiles. However, it's likely the gospel had already reached Caesarea before Peter arrived, as Acts 8 records Phillip "preaching in all the towns until he reached Caesarea" (Acts 8:40).

In any case, an angel appeared to Cornelius, a God-fearing Gentile, and told him to send for Peter, who was staying in Joppa. Cornelius sent three men to retrieve Peter. At the same time, the Lord prepared Peter in a vision to go with these men, telling him to "accompany them without misgivings, for I have sent them Myself" (Acts 10:20).

After a two-day journey, Peter and his companions arrived and entered Cornelius' house. There, Peter proclaimed the gospel to a house full of Cornelius' relatives. After they heard the message, the Holy Spirit came upon them with miraculous manifestations. They believed, and Peter commanded them to be baptized (Acts 10:1–48).

Peter remained there for a few days before departing, to help the new church get started. Perhaps Peter's traveling companions stayed longer or returned later to further strengthen the church. Phillip, among other believers, was already in Caesarea and would probably also have been available to help build up the church and equip their leaders.

To Antioch: Going Without the Apostles

This pattern happened in Jerusalem, Judea and Samaria. Then it exploded to the ends of the earth, not only through the apostles but also through new believers who received Christ through the apostles' ministries and obeyed the Great Commission.

So then those who were scattered because of the persecution that occurred in connection with Stephen, made their way to Phoenicia, and Cyprus and Antioch, speaking the word to no one but to Jews alone. But there were some of them, men of Cyprus and Cyrene, who came to Antioch and began speaking to Greeks also, preaching the Lord Jesus. And the hand of the Lord was with them, and a large number turned to the Lord (Acts 11:19–21).

Notice some key features of the formation of the church in Antioch. First, the apostles stayed in Jerusalem while the other believers scattered to do the Great Commission. Second, these new believers apparently baptized the people they led to faith during this time—and trained others to do the same thing. Third, they trained new believers to start churches where they would grow and obey the Scripture together.

The formation and full functioning of the new churches depended on the laity. There was a significant gap between the time these believers left Jerusalem until the time Barnabas was sent to Antioch. This demonstrates both the autonomy of the developing churches and the efforts of the established church to strengthen and equip them.

Finally, the Holy Spirit called people to go to new areas.

Christ's Power amid Persecution

The story of Acts tells how the Spirit worked through Christ's followers to multiply the gospel from Jerusalem to the ends of the earth (Acts 1:8). The subplot of Acts is how Christ demonstrated His power, verifying the gospel message and proving His faithful presence to the disciples. Despite persecution and opposition—and often spurred on by them—the Great Commission progressed toward fulfillment.

When persecution intensified, so did the joy of the disciples and their resolve to fulfill the Great Commission. Having been beaten and threatened by the religious leaders who conspired to crucify Christ, they rejoiced that they were counted worthy to suffer for His name (Acts 5:40–42). Christ's powerful presence reminded His followers that they had a hope worth living for and a cause worth dying for.

Even when facing martyrdom, disciples experienced the presence of the risen Christ. Stephen saw the glory of God and the Lord standing at His right hand (Acts 7:56). The martyrdom of Stephen and James (the first martyred apostle) could not hinder the advance of the gospel (Acts 7:54–60; 12:2).

Supernatural rescues and miracles sustained the disciples on many occasions, freeing them to continue proclaiming the gospel. The apostles who were released from prison by an angel returned to proclaiming the gospel in the temple (Acts 5:17–21). The church prayed for Peter the night before he was to be martyred, and God rescued him (Acts 12:3–12; 16:22–30). Paul was raised up, having been stoned in Lystra, to take the gospel to Derbe (Acts 14:19–20). Undaunted by his stoning, he soon returned to Lystra with Barnabas to proclaim Christ and strengthen the disciples (Acts 14:21). Later, the Lord answered the prayers of Paul and Silas with an earthquake that freed them from prison (Acts 12:3–12; 16:22–30).

Persecuting Christ's church proved to be a perilous endeavor for the persecutors themselves. Judas the betrayer hanged himself. Acts records the gruesome details of what happened next: "and falling headlong, he burst open in the middle and all his intestines gushed out" (Acts 1:18). God also had the last word with Herod, a notable persecutor. He was struck by an angel of the Lord and died a horrible death after refusing to give God glory after a speech. Luke tells us: "He was eaten by worms and died. But the word of the Lord continued to grow and to be multiplied" (Acts 12:23–24).

The persecutors dealt a blow to the church, but the final, fatal blow was divinely meted out to them.

This truth endures today. Believers in high-security areas are often persecuted to varying degrees because of their faith. Even so, they've learned to celebrate persecution, just as the apostles did in Acts 5:41. These believers say the persecution they faced was an important part of God making them able ministers of the Great Commission. Many times, they also testify of the Lord's supernatural protection.

10. Apostolic Teams Launch *Plan A* Worldwide

The church in Antioch became a launching pad. As they sent apostolic teams[20] on three journeys, entire provinces throughout the Roman Empire were discipled. "The Holy Spirit said, 'Set apart for Me Barnabas and Saul for the work to which I have called them'" (Acts 13:2). The church obeyed, sending out Barnabas and Saul (Paul), and later Paul and Silas.

The following sections show how these three journeys succeeded.[21] Pay attention—do you see the ABIDES pattern?

Highlights of the First Journey: First Provinces Discipled and Churched

Cyprus and Pisidia: First Stops, First Fruit

The first journey began as Paul and Barnabas were sent out by the Holy Spirit to Cyprus. The gospel was proclaimed in synagogues throughout the island. Among those who believed in Cyprus was the proconsul, who came to faith after hearing the gospel and witnessing a miracle of judgment toward a false prophet who opposed the apostolic team (Acts 13:5-12).

Afterward, they proceeded to Antioch in Pisidia. They proclaimed the gospel first to Jews and God-fearers in synagogues, and also to the Gentiles (Acts 13:5, 7–12, 29–41, 47). The responsiveness of the Gentiles in Pisidia is notable: "… and as many as had been appointed to eternal life believed. And the word of the Lord was being spread through the whole region" (Acts 13:48–49). Their multiplication is recorded, even after Paul's and Barnabas' departure: "The disciples [of Pisidia] were continually filled with joy and with the Holy Spirit" (Acts 13:52). The believers became churches.

---

20   Chapter 17 is a practical guide for sending apostolic teams to do Plan A.

21   Mark Stevens deserves credit for developing much of the material related to the ABIDES pattern in Paul's missionary journeys.

As usual, Paul or members of his team later returned to Pisidia to further equip churches and their leaders (Acts 14:21–24). Barnabas and Mark also returned to Cyprus before Paul's second missionary journey (Acts 15:39).

Galatia: Persecution, Power, Productivity

From Pisidian Antioch, the apostolic team entered the province of Galatia in Iconium. They relied on the Lord and spent a long time there proclaiming God's Word. A number of both Jews and Greeks believed. The Holy Spirit's work was evident as many signs and wonders took place, especially in Iconium and Lystra. Because of persecution, they were often forced to advance to the next site, proclaiming the gospel in the surrounding cities and regions (Acts 14:1–20).

After proclaiming the gospel and making many disciples in Derbe, the team returned to strengthen and encourage the disciples in the primary cities where they'd already planted churches. There they appointed elders in every church, commending them to the Lord (Acts 14:21–23), a pattern reiterated by Paul in Titus 1:5.

The fact that the team returned to every church appointing elders underlines the indigenous nature of church planting in Acts. First, groups of newly baptized believers immediately gathered into churches to obey all the commands of Scripture. Second, they were churches before they had appointed elders/overseers. The new believers were all priests who had full authority to obey the whole Scripture. Third, they didn't depend on outside leadership, remaining churches even when the apostolic team departed, which was sometimes quickly. Our job is to go, baptize and teach—and the new believers' job is to believe the gospel, be baptized and be the church.

Still, note that the apostolic team made an effort to return to every place to equip the churches, and both help appoint and train their overseers.

Later, Paul wrote a letter to the Galatian churches to encourage them and their leaders to stay true to the gospel and to walk by the Spirit in grace, rather than being drawn into legalism. Paul also returned to Galatia early in his third missionary journey. The Galatians' progress in the faith and evangelism is recorded as follows: "So the churches were being strengthened in the faith, and were increasing in number daily" (Acts 16:5).

Timothy, a convert from the Galatian province, later joined Paul's apostolic team (Acts 16:1–3) as did others such as Gaius from Derbe.

Highlights of the Second Journey: Provinces of Macedonia and Achaia Discipled and Churched

Macedonia: Three Primary Breakthroughs in Several Months

Among the several church-planting breakthroughs in the province of Macedonia, three occurrences are most noteworthy. And these breakthroughs happened in a relatively short time frame. Paul and Silas stayed perhaps a month in Philippi and another month in Thessalonica.[22] In Berea they stayed an unspecified time, perhaps less than two months. In each case churches were planted, resulting in thorough discipleship of the Macedonian province. These churches also contributed full-time members to the larger missionary effort (Acts 20:4).

Philippi

During this initial visit to Philippi, Paul and Silas reached two families who became the foundation for spreading the gospel throughout the entire province.

The Spirit of Jesus didn't allow Paul and Silas to go to Bithynia, but rather guided them to Macedonia through a vision (Acts 16:7–10). There they proclaimed the gospel to a group of women in Philippi, who had assembled by the riverside on the Sabbath. From the group, Lydia responded to the good news. It appears she also ensured that her household heard the gospel, as they were baptized together (Acts 16:14–15). After this, Paul and Silas stayed at Lydia's house for a short time. By all appearances, this resulted in a church in Lydia's house (Acts 16:40).

A separate event during this time led to another significant development in Philippi. Paul and Silas were beaten and imprisoned for casting a demon out of a slave girl (Acts 16:16–24). This proved to be a divinely prepared opportunity.

---

22   Paul reasoned in the synagogue for three Sabbaths (Acts 17:2). Paul and Silas may have stayed a while longer in Thessalonica, as Paul received support more than once from the Philippians during his time in Thessalonica (Phil. 4:16).

As they were praying and singing in jail, an earthquake allowed for the potential escape of the prisoners. But instead of leaving, Paul and Silas, along with the other inmates, remained there and proclaimed the gospel to the jailer. Notice their response to the jailer's question, "Sirs, what must I do be saved?" (Acts 16:30). Paul and Silas answered in a way that encouraged multiplication. "They said, 'Believe in the Lord Jesus, and you will be saved, you and your household'" (Acts 16:31).

Indeed, the jailer gathered his household to hear the gospel, they believed and were baptized and became part of the church in Philippi.

The Magistrates then forced Paul and Silas to leave Philippi. However, they had already demonstrated how to live as disciples of Christ (Phil. 3:17).

The letter to the Philippians is part of Paul's ongoing effort to develop the church and equip church leaders in Philippi and the rest of Macedonia. Moreover, Paul and his co-workers returned to the area to strengthen the believers (Acts 18:5; 20:1–5). The Philippian believers also became involved in Paul's ministry, as several times they supported his work, both in Thessalonica and outside of the province of Macedonia (Phil. 4:10–19). Paul commended them because of their participation in the gospel from day one (Phil. 1:5).

Thessalonica

Still in the province of Macedonia, Paul and Silas passed through Amphipolis and Apollonia to the city of Thessalonica. During their brief stay, they started a church that would have a part in discipling not only Macedonia but Achaia. The Thessalonians' example of transformed lives and zeal eventually caused Paul to write, "Finally brethren, pray for us that the word of the Lord will spread rapidly and be glorified, just as it did also with you" (2 Thess. 3:1). Of course, Paul desired for word to spread rapidly in other areas he served, just as it happened in Thessalonica! Luke's record of their time in Thessalonica is brief (Acts 17:1–9). However, Paul's letters to the Thessalonian church clarify the pattern and motivate his readers to spread the gospel while growing deeper in their walk with Christ.

Paul and Silas proclaimed the gospel (Acts 17:3). A large number of God-fearing Greeks, a number of the leading women and some Jews professed faith (Acts 17:4). We assume they were baptized immediately, as there's no evidence to suggest they diverted from the normal pattern.

Upset by this, some wicked men and Jews from the synagogue formed a mob and attacked the house of Jason, perhaps the meeting place of a new house church. Jason and other new believers were dragged before the authorities, but later released.

Paul's letters to the church in Thessalonica show how the church developed and how its leaders were equipped. Although Satan blocked Paul and his co-workers from going back to Thessalonica (1 Thess. 2:17–18), Timothy was finally able to return to strengthen and encourage the believers there (1 Thess. 3:2).

Many Thessalonian believers introduced the gospel to new places. The Word of the Lord sounded forth from them into Macedonia, Achaia and everywhere they went (1 Thess. 1:8).

Berea

After Paul and his co-workers were sent away by night from Thessalonica, they ministered in Berea. The Bereans were eager to hear the Word, so they studied the Scriptures daily and many of them believed. Afterward, Paul was escorted to Athens (Acts 17:15) while Silas and Timothy remained in Berea for a time to encourage and strengthen the newly planted church.

Strategy-Based, Not Schedule-Based

No matter how long the apostolic team was going to be in any area, they implemented a similar strategy with the same sense of urgency. They immediately attempted to lead people to faith by proclaiming the gospel, baptizing them and gathering new believers to form churches where they were discipled and trained.

The team may suddenly have to leave, but the Holy Spirit would remain to continue the work. In addition, members of the apostolic team would soon return to guide the new believers through the stages of church development, leadership training and facilitating the spread of the gospel through the local church to new areas. Dedicated believers from these churches often joined Paul's larger missionary team, either engaging new peoples, or helping with the development of previously planted churches. Aristarchus of Macedonia, Secundus and Sopater are examples of this.

Achaia

Christ's presence was obvious to Paul in Corinth, as the Lord said to him in a vision: "Do not be afraid any longer, but go on speaking and do not be silent; for I am with you, and no man will attack you in order to harm you, for I have many people in this city" (Acts 18:9–10). Therefore, Paul stayed in Corinth for a year and a half. New believers reached others with the gospel. They formed churches and their churches and leaders were equipped, as evidenced by Paul's letter to the Corinthian church.

Aquila and Priscilla joined Paul's team in Corinth. From Corinth they were placed in Ephesus, where they planted a church that met in their house (1 Cor. 16:19), as they did later in Rome as well (Romans 16:3-5a). While in Ephesus, they also further discipled Apollos, who returned to Achaia as an evangelist and encourager to the churches (Acts 18:24-28).

The sending of Aquila and Priscilla was one way the Corinthian church implemented the Great Commission in other areas. Paul desired for the Corinthian church to participate in enlarging the reach of his gospel ministry to the regions beyond themselves (2 Cor. 10:15–16).

Great Commission Baptismal Pattern Demonstrated in Achaia

Paul baptized only two individuals and one family in the province of Achaia, yet his ministry was instrumental in the discipling of the entire province. Why did Paul choose to baptize only three parties, even though he was available to baptize more? First, he wanted to avoid conflict in the churches over which "big" religious figure baptized them. Second, he knew the importance of transferring baptismal responsibilities to each new believer.

Look at what he writes to the church at Corinth, the capital city of Achaia:

> I thank God I baptized none of you except Crispus and Gaius, so that no one would say you were baptized in my name. Now I did baptize also the household of Stephanas; beyond that, I do not know whether I baptized any other (1 Cor. 1:14–16).

When Paul entered the province of Achaia, he reached and baptized the household of Stephanas. They were the "first fruits of Achaia," as stated in his letter to the Corinthian church (1 Cor. 16:15–16).

Paul baptized the very first family who believed in the province of Achaia, but not those they led to faith. Responsibility for baptism transferred immediately from Paul to the new local believers.

As Paul entered Corinth, he reached and baptized Crispus, the first believer there: "Crispus, the leader of the synagogue, believed in the Lord with all of his household, and many of the Corinthians when they heard believed and were baptized" (Acts 18:8). According to Paul, he only baptized Crispus. And apparently, he was the only outsider with Crispus at this time.[23]

Who baptized the others? Crispus likely baptized his family, since Paul didn't. Local believers, probably including Crispus, baptized those they later led to faith. Paul also reached and baptized Gaius, but none of his associates. This is apparently the person of whom it is said, "Gaius, host to me and to the whole church, greets you" (Rom. 16:23). As the first convert in his family, it appears that Gaius would have baptized those he reached with the gospel.

Baptism Strategy in Paul's Ministry

Acts demonstrates that Paul's church planting pattern included immediately transferring the responsibility for baptism to those new believers who had themselves been baptized.

However, Paul emphasized that he preferred for someone other than himself to baptize, so that new believers wouldn't be proud of who baptized them (1 Cor. 1:14-15). Who baptized new believers wasn't important. What was important is that they were baptized, obeying Christ's first command to them by acknowledging their profession of faith in the death and resurrection of Jesus Christ.

---

23   Paul was accompanied in Corinth at this time by Silas and Timothy, but it appears that Paul alone ministered to Crispus. Either way, Paul baptized Crispus, but not his family and the others who believed as the result of his ministry.

Highlights of the Third Journey: Province of Asia Minor Discipled and Churched

Asia Minor: Training Disciples to Disciple an Entire Province

Eventually, Paul made it to Ephesus in Asia Minor, having previously been forbidden by the Spirit from going there (Acts 16:6). First, he met twelve followers of John the Baptist, explained to them more fully about Jesus and the Holy Spirit and then baptized them. Paul proclaimed the gospel for a three-month period. Those who believed were doubtlessly baptized and became churches, although it isn't explicitly stated in the text. When persecution arose, Paul transitioned from teaching in the synagogue to teaching in the school of Tyrannus.

There he taught believers daily for two years, emphasizing both deep discipleship and intentional obedience to the Great Commission. The results were astounding: "This took place for two years, so that all who lived in Asia (the province of Asia Minor) heard the word of the Lord, both Jews and Greeks" (Acts 19:10). Paul used the school building as a training center for discipling and equipping new believers.

A strong church developed throughout the region of Ephesus, as evidenced by Paul's letter to the Ephesian church. Paul's two letters to Timothy, a member of Paul's team who ministered for a time in Ephesus, also explain the development of the Ephesian church. It had a strong base of elders-overseers as evidenced in Paul's farewell address to them (Acts 20).

More is known about leadership development in the Ephesian church than in any other church. In his farewell to the elders in Ephesus, Paul revealed how he related to them. For three years Paul equipped the elders-overseers of the Ephesian church publicly and from house to house. He endured hardship and often shed tears for their spiritual well-being. His integrity was apparent, as he didn't covet their possessions. Instead, he worked hard to supply his own needs and the needs of his team. He taught and admonished them day and night. He warned them about false teachers and prepared them to face down falsehood. Finally, Paul commended the overseers of the Ephesian churches to God and His word (Acts 20:18–35).

Another characteristic of the Ephesian church was its faithfulness in sending out missionaries. This church is likely responsible for planting churches in Colossae and other places. Epaphras, from the Ephesian church, shared the gospel with those who became the church at Colossae (Col. 1:5–8). It seems probable that the churches in Laodicea and Hierapolis also were started by believers from Ephesus (Col. 4:12–13). Epaphras and others, such as Tychicus and Trophimus, ultimately devoted themselves fully to Great Commission work, joining Paul's missionary team (Acts 20:4).

Summary of the Pattern in Acts

Several facts are apparent about the apostolic team's strategy in each place. First, they depended on the Holy Spirit. Second, they were committed to evangelize all peoples. Third, they took seriously Jesus' command to baptize new believers. Where people proved responsive to the gospel, they formed churches. The team either stayed, or efficiently returned to develop the churches and their leaders. The churches were committed to implementing *Plan A* in nearby areas. And the apostolic team moved on, aided by the churches and believers from each province, to apply *Plan A* in other unreached areas.

When the gospel message was rejected, the apostolic team "shook off the dust" and set out to find those who would receive the gospel (as in Acts 13:51; 18:6, etc.). Remember the A.B.I.D.E.S. acrostic from the beginning of Chapter 9. How does it apply to what we've just learned?

- **Abide** in Christ: The apostles and other believers were living by the Spirit.

- **Bold Evangelism**: They proclaimed the gospel and led people to Christ. New believers were baptized either by the believer who reached them or someone else who attended at that time.

- **Instill Multiplication**: New believers were expected to immediately begin reaching their family, friends and acquaintances. Those reached were baptized either by or with the ones who reached them.

- **Develop Churches:** The new believers were taught how to worship together as a church—usually in one of their homes—and to continue reaching and discipling those from their oikos (family, friends and other relationships) and those in close proximity to them. Simultaneously, they reached others who also formed churches.

- **Equip Churches and their Leaders:** As groups and churches formed, leaders emerged from the congregations and were appointed because of their character and faithful service. The churches and their leaders received ongoing discipleship and training either directly from the apostolic team, or through subsequent contact through letters and visits from members of the apostolic team.[24] For example, the teaching of teachers became one of Timothy's primary assignments (2 Tim. 2:2).

- **Send Believers to New Areas to Repeat the Process:** Believers naturally and intentionally repeated the process as they went to new areas. In addition to going, they financially supported and prayed for others. Those who were sent reported back how the gospel was advancing so the church would be encouraged and further involved in both the local and worldwide commission. It is also noteworthy that in every area where the church developed, some believers from those areas joined the larger missionary team, devoting themselves wholly to Great Commission fulfillment.

---

24   For instance, there are five "prophets and teachers" listed in the Antioch church (Acts 13:1), including Barnabas and Saul. However, upon their return from the first missionary journey, many others also were teaching and preaching the word of the Lord (Acts 15:35).

Part Four: Developing Priests, Churches and Leaders

11. We Really Are Real Priests

Almost all Protestant denominations hold to the doctrine of the priesthood of the believer. But what would happen if we actually practiced this doctrine? The goal of bringing every person who believes the gospel to full maturity in Christ depends on it.

Jesus' Kingdom of Priests

> But you are a chosen race, a royal priesthood, a holy nation, a people for God's own possession, so that you may proclaim the excellencies of Him who has called you out of darkness into His marvelous light (1 Peter 2:9).

Fresh Priesthood

In the Mosaic Law (Torah), only Levites were designated as priests. Only they had the right to do priestly duties. When Jesus came, He introduced a new age in which He was the Chief Priest. He delegated priestly duties to His followers, under His authority. Jesus, however, wasn't a Levite; He was from the tribe of Judah. He was introducing a fresh, new priesthood.

Flat Priesthood

Jesus is the one and only great High Priest (Heb. 4:14–5:10). Traditional church models often refer to a hierarchical priesthood from Jesus to the apostles and others appointed by the apostles. However, Jesus enacted a priesthood that was transferrable from Himself to every new believer through the presence of the Holy Spirit. In other words, Jesus implemented a "flat," rather than hierarchical, priesthood with every Spirit-indwelled believer as a priest.

A hierarchical priesthood would make the Great Commission difficult. Whenever a new believer sees himself as always and only a student, dependence on the discipler often results. Certainly, the new believer will be inferior in knowledge and often in skills to the person who reached him. However, by teaching the new believer that they're a partner-priest, he or she learns to do, rather than passively watch and pray.

The Great Commission is also short-circuited if new believers don't take up their priestly duties. This can happen because of disobedience, but it often happens because the authority and responsibility of every believer's priesthood is never understood.

Contrary to popular opinion, recognizing one's priesthood doesn't elevate status or inflate self-esteem. The primary purpose of being a priest is to do the Christ's priestly works. Priests fulfill necessary roles that serve God's purposes. Any other benefit of being a priest is secondary. Priests serve at Christ's disposal.

Functional Priesthood

In established churches, the long-standing pattern is for clergy to do the work of the ministry, while the laity supports them prayerfully and financially. The clergy are seen as priests over non-priest church members. Biblically however, all believers are priests and all believers are set aside to do the work of the ministry.

Interestingly, the Bible identifies church leaders as shepherds (*poimen*), overseers (*episkopos*) and elders (*presbuteros*), but never as priests (*hiereus*). All Christians, however, are called priests before God. Too often, only the pastor and pastoral staff actually function as priests. Even though both clergy and laity accept the priesthood of all believers as a doctrine, they act as if priestly duties are reserved for ordained clergy only.

Let us now consider the characteristics and tasks of believer-priests. Notice in particular those duties related to obeying the Great Commission.

Serve as a Priest

The following section gives an overview of priestly functions. Biblically, the following functions aren't limited to overseers of churches (pastors, clergy, etc.), but are expected to be carried out by ordinary believers within the body of Christ. However, that doesn't mean each believer will perform all these functions. For instance, not every believer will be a recognized pastor, and it's likely not every believer will have the opportunity to lead the Lord's Supper.

Corporately speaking, however, we're able to do all the functions necessary to fulfill the Great Commission and be the church.

Pray Confidently (Heb. 4:14-16; 10:19-22)

Pray Intimately through Christ

What's the advantage of having a High Priest who has already lived through, and successfully endured, all we will ever experience? In Old Testament times, only the High Priest could enter the most holy room of the temple, and then only once a year. But according to the passages above, our rights as priests are better than those of the Old Testament priests! How? Our great High Priest gives authority and His indwelling presence for priestly tasks.

As priests, we should have set times of prayer in which we intercede for others. We also should set aside time to pray for people's needs and the spread of the gospel. This approach to prayer proves that Christians love not only each other, but lost people as well.

Pray Intentionally with Others

Christians are accustomed to saying, "I'll pray for you." However, it's often better to say, "Let's pray" or "Let me pray with you." Praying on the spot demonstrates Christ's presence with us and invites Christ to answer. Like evangelism itself, prayer should be happening with anyone, anywhere and at any time.

We often pray for people on the spot, even in public or high security places. In these situations, we don't have to close our eyes or change our posture. We simply talk to the Lord Jesus, who is always with us.

Reach the Lost with the Gospel

> But I've written very boldly to you on some points, so as to remind you again, because of the grace that was given me from God, to be a minister of Christ Jesus to the Gentiles, ministering as a priest the gospel of God, so that my offering of the Gentiles may become acceptable, sanctified by the Holy Spirit (Romans 15:15–16).

In the Torah, a priest was considered a mediator between God and man. Old Testament priests offered blood sacrifices to atone for people's sins and to make peace between man and God. Christ as our great high priest has accomplished that for us—fully and finally. So how does our job as priests mirror the Old Testament priest's task of helping people make peace with God?

The answer is simple: every believer should share the gospel. From the beginning, new believers should associate sharing the gospel with the Christian life. But complicated evangelism methods are difficult to model and transfer to others. This is why we should train new believers with simple evangelism methods. Having seen it themselves, the new converts can quickly master it.

People can only be saved as they surrender themselves to Jesus Christ and believe in both His sacrifice for our sins and in His resurrection. People can only believe the gospel if they hear the gospel, and they can only hear the gospel if we're faithful in proclaiming it (Romans 10:13–15).

Illustrate the Gospel through Baptism and the Lord's Supper

Priests proclaim the gospel of Christ. They're also expected to baptize and serve the Lord's Supper, both of which picture the gospel for believers. Baptism illustrates the new believer's identification with Christ's death and resurrection. Although believers aren't saved by baptism, baptism represents the "front door" of the church, the beginning of a believer's walk with Christ.

The Lord's Supper also symbolizes the gospel, emphasizing the sacrificial death of Christ. It continually reminds believers of their allegiance to Him, and their commitment to proclaim the gospel until He comes. That command should be obeyed by baptized believers together as soon as possible.

Baptism

What happens next after the gospel has been shared and someone believes and confesses "Jesus Christ is Lord" (Rom. 10.9-10)? According to the Bible, the answer should almost always be baptism. Usually this is done immediately and in relationship to membership in a church, either an already existing one or a new one.

Lord's Supper

According to Acts 2:42, 46, the followers of Christ were "breaking bread" together. That phrase has two possible meanings. First, it was a natural phrase for eating together. However, Acts 2:46 states that the Christians were breaking bread and also taking their meals together. This probably differentiates "breaking bread" from merely "eating together." Second, as is likely in this context, the phrase referred specifically to the Lord's Supper. It appears the early disciples of Christ routinely celebrated the Lord's Supper together, to remember and proclaim Christ's sacrificial death until He returns.

However, the apostles didn't always attend, so who led the observance in their house groups? The believers themselves did.

Requirements for the Lord's Supper are given in two passages: Luke 22:14–19 and 1 Corinthians 11:17–34. No limitations are given for who may administer the Lord's Supper. Rather, the requirements are given so participants will live in unity and obedience to Scripture, and so they will confess sin and make relationships right before partaking.

Lord's Supper Requirements

1. Done when believers are gathered together (church ordinance).
2. Done with two elements that represent Christ's sacrifice (bread and cup).
3. Done with regularity.
4. Done in a worthy manner (without factions, rightly judging the body, submission to one another).
5. Done after self-examination and purification.
6. Done to remember the Lord's death.
7. Done to proclaim the Lord's death until He comes.

Equip and Expand the Body of Christ

Priests equip other believers to grow in Christ-likeness and works of service. Every believer is endowed with gifts for building up the body of Christ (1 Cor. 12–14). Some believers are particularly gifted to equip others to do so (Eph. 4:11–13). By equipping others in the work of the ministry, believer-priests multiply themselves through each new believer they disciple and train, and the multiplication continues as those new believers do the same.

The apostles and prophets laid a solid foundation for Christ's church to expand (Eph. 2:19–21). They became the blocks upon which the church was built. First, they were inspired to write the New Testament. Second, they initiated our obedience to the commands of the Great Commission. With Jesus as the cornerstone, the apostles became the foundation for the first generation of new believers—and for succeeding generations as well.

Sanctify Yourself (Rom. 12:1–2)

In the past, priests wore special clothes to identify themselves as holy. Today, believer-priests aren't known by their special clothes, but rather by their holy deeds. They surrender to Christ's Lordship to pursue sanctification (Heb. 12:14).

The Spirit sanctifies obedient believer priests. In the process, He not only He not only makes us priests; He makes us holy priests. Believers continually surrender themselves to Christ to become holy and be filled with the Spirit.

Teach God's Word (2 Tim. 2:2)

In most religions, an elite group of teachers (priests) have the sole right to interpret their holy books. In other words, they hold the keys, while average adherents passively receive what their teachers say, right or wrong. Often, the laity are discouraged, or even forbidden, from studying the holy books apart from the priest's tutelage. This is also true among false teachers, even those claiming to be Christian.

The truth and authority of Christianity are found in the Bible—not in the views of those who teach it. In Acts, even as people are coming to faith, they're encouraged to study the Bible. The Bereans were commended that "they received the word with great eagerness, examining the Scriptures daily to see whether these things were so" (Acts. 17:11).

Believer-priests can understand the Bible. The Holy Spirit teaches believers (John 14:26) and guides them into all truth (John 16:13). Led by the Spirit, believers study and know what the Scripture says and means and how to apply it. This is especially so when they study in community (groups and churches).

The Holy Spirit equips faithful believers to teach others what He has taught them through others (2 Tim. 2:2). In a general sense, everyone teaches one another what they're learning from the Scripture. They all point others to the Scripture as their source of authority and comfort. However, God only calls some as recognized shepherds and "teachers" who equip the believers (Eph. 4:11–12, James 3:1).

12. Leaders, Equippers and Servants of the Priests

Church leaders serve a vital role in fulfilling the Great Commission. They serve the congregation by equipping them as priests.

Leading and Equipping

Leaders emerge within the churches. Often, these leaders are then appointed as overseers, synonymously called elders and shepherds. Qualifications for this office are spelled out in 1 Timothy 3:1-7 and Titus 1:5-9. What's remarkable about those appointed as overseers is how unremarkable they are. Rather simply, they paint the picture of mature Christian men who excel in teaching. Everything else is part and parcel of compliance with standard Christian discipleship and sanctification.

Teachers provide "on the job" training to the newly appointed overseers, teaching them how to equip their local churches. In the New Testament, letters to the churches often contain advice for both the entire churches and their overseers. The letters were read publicly to ensure mutual accountability. In the same way, there are no "secret" lessons for leaders that aren't also shared with the entire church; the overseers are to remain laity.

These appointed overseers lead, equip, and guide the teaching of the churches in sound doctrine and Great Commission obedience. The result is that all believers of the church are equipped for every good work, maturing in Christ (Eph. 4:12–16). Church leaders were never meant to become high priests to their congregations. Every Christ-follower has the right and responsibility to serve as a priest. Church leaders are simply responsible to lead and to equip others to serve well.

In first-century church planting, leaders (elders)[25] were appointed in every church (Acts 14:23) and in every city (Titus 1:5). These two

---

25   The plural "elders" could refer to either plural elders in each local church or the sum of all the elders serving an area where churches exist. Either way, leaders were accountable to their congregations and shared leadership responsibilities and decision-making.

phrases, "every church" and "every city" are perhaps synonymous. The apostolic team worked with groups of baptized believers, who were already functioning as churches, to appoint biblically qualified leaders.

Again, qualified leaders for new churches must meet the standards set forth in Scripture. In other words, they're not automatically elders just because they were among the ones who originally gathered the group. Over time, faithful members often arise who are more qualified and gifted to shepherd the church, so they are appointed as the overseers.

Since all are priests, how do church leaders relate to church members? First, the elders are the appointed leaders. They've been appointed to oversee, shepherd and impart wisdom as elders.

It is important not to confuse the priesthood—which includes every Christian—and the pastorate—which is only appropriate for specific Christians appointed for that ministry. Priesthood is about function, not having authority over others. Qualified leaders emerge and are recognized and appointed from among the believer-priests. They lead by example, setting the tone for ministry and serving as a role model for those they shepherd.

The appointed leaders weren't recognized in order for them to do priestly duties, but because they'd already done them well. They were appointed because of their character, not their talents. Even so, the primary skill necessary for overseers (elders) was the ability "to exhort in sound doctrine and to refute those who contradict" (Titus 1:9). Appointing leaders from within the congregation eliminates the gap between clergy and laity, while fostering a sense of working together to see Christ's kingdom come.

Church leaders are stewards of the body's gifts.[26] They equip believers and enable them to mature in their faith. The equipping role of the leader is essential both for the fulfillment of the mission and the development of healthy churches. Church leaders become roadblocks if they do ministry by themselves and therefore fail to equip and send others.

Serving

All appointed church leaders are servants who minister to believers by leading and equipping. In addition to recognized church overseers,

---

26   I first heard this statement from Dr. Elmer Towns at Liberty University in 1987.

other servants are appointed to fulfill more specialized needs of the congregation; these are often called deacons.

As churches grow, needs arise that require the appointment of servants (*diakonos*) to serve the needs of the congregation. The qualifications for those who serve in these roles are listed in 1 Timothy 3:8–13. The appointment of servants might be required to meet physical needs, as in the Jerusalem church (Acts 6:1–6).

Specially designated servants may also assist in endeavors and meet broader ministry needs than those of just one local church. For example, designated representatives of local networks often accompanied Paul's apostolic teams to help advance the gospel throughout the world. It's imperative that these servants are people of character, who are fully on board with a biblical church planting vision.

Avoid Hierarchical Network Leadership Structures

Frequently, unappointed leaders emerge who serve the needs of the broader community of churches. These leaders arise from among the overseers of local churches. Unlike local church leaders, however, network leaders don't have positional authority in the larger community of churches. Appointed local church leaders have leadership authority within their local church, even though their primary role is equipping. There are no examples in Acts of authoritative leadership hierarchies outside the local church.

The Jerusalem Council (Acts 15:13–30) affirms the right of local churches and networks to self-govern without the burden of hierarchical imposition. Although the Judaizers tried to enslave the new churches with extra-biblical bondage, the Jerusalem Council simply requested new churches to obey the guidelines of Scripture, while acknowledging the customs of the Jewish believers around them. When that word reached the new churches, "they rejoiced because of its encouragement" (Acts 15:31).

Hierarchies usually impose extra-biblical rules upon churches. They limit the autonomy of the local church and therefore undermine the priesthood of believers and hinder the progress of the gospel.

13. Believers Prepared to Teach Others to Be the Church

Don't Take Them to Church–Make Them a Church

Believers have three Great Commission tasks: go, baptize and teach them to obey all Christ's commands. Similarly, unbelievers also have three tasks: believe the gospel, be baptized and be the church! Although various kinds of believer groups can form in the process of Great Commission obedience, the goal is to start churches, not simply groups.

When new believers are reached near an existing church, they're often integrated into that church. But when a nearby biblical church doesn't yet exist, the next step is to plant one. The new believers there are the first member(s) of the church in that area—or among their people group. After the initial stage of receiving the gospel and being gathered into a body, the church will be guided through a discipleship process that leads to spiritual maturity.

Discipleship in Groups/Churches

As soon as groups of baptized believers identify themselves as the local body of Christ and commit to regularly meet to obey all the commands of Scripture, they become churches.

Discipleship rarely happens in a vacuum, nor was it intended to. Discipleship is meant to take place in churches. When believers learn and obey the Bible together in community, illumined and guided by the Holy Spirit, they become mature disciples in strong churches.[27]

What nourishes new churches over time? An unswerving adherence and Spirit-led obedience to Scripture. The Bible alone is God's infallible Word, and its content must be at the foundation of every church. In this way, the Spirit sanctifies new believers by His Word. And as they apply the Word, they experience the peace and power of the Spirit's leadership.

---

27   Church definition and development are further discussed in Chapter 15.

Radically Biblical First and Twenty-First Century Churches

Jesus tells us, "I will build my church" (Matt. 16:18). Among many things, this means church membership is non-negotiable for Christians. From the early church on, once new believers were baptized, they were considered members of the body of Christ—universally, but also locally. In Acts, church membership characterized those who had been baptized and identified with Christ through repentance and faith.

The churches in Acts seem vastly different from today. The church (ecclesia) was the gathering of a specific people, the called-out ones. Where they met was largely irrelevant, but what they did as a church and their commitment to one another was vital.

Three expressions of the New Testament Church

What is a New Testament Church?

First, a church is a local group of baptized believers who intentionally covenant together under the authority of the Word and the leadership of elders, to help each other follow Jesus and participate in the church's ordinances: baptism and the Lord's Supper. These groups sometimes meet in homes, but they can gather anywhere. Examples of these types of churches are found in Acts 2:37–42, Colossians 4:15 and Philemon 2. In the New Testament, local churches were often house churches, and each local gathering—regardless of size—performed the functions of a local church.

Second, the New Testament also refers to local churches in a specific region as a "church." This would be like us saying "the church of Phoenix, referring to all churches in and around that area. For example, when Paul wrote to the church at Corinth, he apparently was writing to all the local churches, or a network of churches, in Corinth. The same was true of the church in Rome, Galatia, Ephesus and Philippi.

Third, all believers everywhere are corporately called the church. This is the church in the universal sense (Matt. 16:18).

Most often, the word "church" is used to refer to either individual churches or all the local churches in an area.

They're Not All Small

This book focuses on smaller churches (usually house churches) among under-reached peoples and under-reached areas. However, we must also affirm the good work done by larger established churches who have faithfully reached out to the people around them with the gospel.

It's certainly not wrong or unusual for churches to be large. In fact, there are thousands of established churches being used by God to reach their "Jerusalem/ Judea." Churches that begin as house churches might grow and become larger, established churches. Others might merge and form larger churches. The point isn't size, but health. The goal of every church should be to grow locally, while reaching new peoples and places with the intent of starting healthy, multiplying churches there.

What did New Testament churches do?

The phrase "52 Oikos Church" helps us understand the basic functions of New Testament churches.

"5": Churches perform five basic functions, which can be sub-divided into twelve more specific categories.[28] Acts 2:37–42 sets the pattern for what churches do. Churches:

1. study the Word (discipleship and teaching);

2. worship (various forms, including prayer and singing, etc.);

3. fellowship together as members of the body of Christ;

4. minister to those within and without the church; and

5. reach the lost (locally and where the gospel is unknown).

It should also be added that churches practice biblical church discipline. That is, according to scriptural directives, they seek to discipline openly sinful members in order to restore them. However, church discipline can result in expulsion of those who refuse the loving call for repentance and restoration. More on church discipline this can be found in 1 Corinthians 5:1–11 and Matthew 18:15–20.

---

28   The 12 biblical characteristics of healthy churches are as follows: 1) Evangelism 2) Discipleship 3) Membership 4) Leadership 5) Preaching/ Teaching 6) Baptism and Lord's Supper 7) Worship 8) Fellowship 9) Prayer 10) Accountability and Church Discipline 11) Giving and 12) Missions. Foundations, International Mission Board, SBC, 2018, p. 69-72.

"2": Churches practice the two ordinances that are visual testimonies to the gospel—baptism and the Lord's Supper. Churches are comprised of baptized believers who take the Lord's Supper together regularly. These ordinances are the primary distinguishing factors between churches and other occasional groups of Christians, such as Bible study groups.

"52": Churches meet consistently and intend to be a local church. The number 52 represents meeting at least weekly. Since church members are living in community, they often worship together formally and informally throughout the week, as well. In contrast, groups that are not churches might meet sporadically without the clear intention of being a church. In other words, churches covenant together as the body of Christ. Although first-century churches met at least weekly, usually on Sunday, there was no particular day mandated for worship (Rom. 14:5-6).

"Oikos"

New Testament churches often started out as oikos (household) churches, begun with members of a family unit. These churches performed the functions previously described and were led by their members. They also often were part of the larger church body emerging in their area.

STRONG Churches

"STRONG"[29] is a simple acronym used to summarize basic principles of biblical churches:

- **S**ole authority is the Bible
- **T**asks of the church are all being done (5 functions and 2 ordinances)
- **R**eproducing locally and throughout the world
- **O**rdinary believers leading, doing all the duties and deciding together
- **N**ot forsaking the assembly (covenant together and consistent meeting)
- **G**overned locally (autonomous)

---

29   The "STRONG" acronym was originally developed by Mark Stevens.

Who Can Start and Lead a Church?

After an initial time of guiding new believers in discipleship and teaching them how to be the church together, the apostles and other New Testament evangelists would commend those believers to the Lord and leave to reproduce the model in a new area. The field-workers would keep in touch with the developing church, either by returning periodically, sending someone else to observe, or corresponding with the churches through letters.

It's not necessary for new believers to meet certain qualifications before starting churches. Any believer who obeys the Great Commission could succeed in leading others to faith, gathering them together and baptizing them as guided by the mission team. The group obeys the commands of Scripture, becoming a church even while leaders are developing. The churches of Acts already were churches when Paul and his team revisited them to help appoint their leaders (Acts 14:21–23). When church leaders with good character and pastoral gifting emerge, the church will appoint elders, following the guidelines of Titus 1:5-9 and 1 Timothy 3:1-7.

Leaders must be appointed based on biblical qualifications. In many situations, believers prove their calling within a fairly brief time frame. After a period of a few months, Paul's missionary team returned to recently established churches to appoint elders (Acts 14:21-23). The believers have gained spiritual character, foundational biblical knowledge and ministry experience, so they are no longer novices. New believers are prohibited from being appointed as overseers (1 Tim. 3:6). What constitutes "new" will likely vary somewhat according to circumstance. The proof of their ministry, along with the development of their character, will verify leadership qualifications.

14. Church and Leadership Development

A church and its leaders should be continually both going and growing at the same time.

Leadership and church development are intrinsically related. Where leadership development stops, discipleship stops. Leaders are those who have become exemplary disciples, who in turn facilitate exemplary discipleship in churches.

Leaders emerge from among the church membership in the discipleship process. Church leaders aren't appointed so they can perform priestly duties; they are appointed because they've been doing them well.

Leadership development is an outgrowth of healthy discipleship. Also, leadership development doesn't begin once leaders have been identified, but rather from the first days of discipling new believers. In Paul's farewell address to the elders of the Ephesian church, he reminisces about the early days of discipleship, before they were appointed as leaders. "You yourselves know, from the first day that I set foot in Asia, how I was with you the whole time…" These leaders emerged from the many believers Paul was discipling three years before. They became faithful disciples, then they were recognized as elders—exemplary disciples.

It is impossible to know immediately who the appointed leaders will be, so disciple them all as though they have leadership potential. The discipleship process will identify those who have the character, skill and giftedness to be appointed as leaders—but by that time, they're usually already leading.

In the early stages of church development, all believers are receiving the same basic teaching. They are taught to go farther with the gospel, while growing deeper in the Word. Everyone is responsible to obey all the commands of Christ. Therefore, everyone must go (share the gospel) and become obedient disciples in their church. In this process, areas of giftedness do emerge in believer's lives, enabling them to invest their time and talents in various ways to encourage and equip the church.

However, gifted believers who can equip others must be identified and trained for churches to develop healthily.

Paul demonstrated in Ephesus the norm of church and leadership development. After baptizing the first few believers in Ephesus, who gathered the churches there, Paul trained the new believers to proclaim the gospel throughout the province, while simultaneously becoming fully obedient disciples. (Acts 19:8-10). During this time church leaders (elders) were identified and equipped to become overseers of the churches. That is why, when Paul said "good-bye" to the elders of the Ephesian church he reminded them, of this time of public training, as mentioned above.

Remember that there are no "secret lessons" for the leaders. All truth taught to the leaders should be conveyed to the congregations as well. It is no coincidence that letters written to church leaders were also supposed to be read publicly to the churches. That provides mutual accountability and encouragement for both the leaders and their congregations to fulfill their respective roles well.

How does training facilitate leadership development?

Training at 4 Levels

Entry-Level Training

Entry-level training is simply this: the person who reaches a new believer begins training them in the basics of the Christian faith—everything from theology to spiritual disciplines like prayer, Bible reading and personal evangelism. Every new believer starts their training right away, even as they begin to grow in the faith.

Church-Level Training

Members of churches meet together to grow in grace as they study the word together. As they study, they teach one another and build one another up. As church leaders with teaching gifts are recognized by the church, these further equip the body of Christ to understand the Word and apply it.

Church Network-Level Training

As churches emerge, gifted teachers—usually from among the church's overseers—are identified and trained to nurture leaders of other churches, and through these leaders to nurture their local churches. In network-level training, an outside teacher (at first)[30] trains teachers from inside emerging networks. In turn, these inside teachers train group leaders from their respective networks.

Big-Group Training

Occasional big-group training events, even after the early stages of church planting can be held for the purposes of fellowship or solving problems that arise. Getting many leaders together builds synergy and a sense of being part of something larger than the separate groups.

Publicly and from House to House

Discipleship and training are done both in homes and in larger groups. As long as it's feasible, it's most practical to proclaim the gospel and train disciples in larger groups. However, when a community becomes divided based on their response to the gospel, believers often are no longer able to gather in larger groups. At that point, training transitions primarily to the homes—both to avoid undue persecution and for practical reasons.

Security concerns may play a role in where training takes place. Security, however, shouldn't be our primary concern. After the apostles were beaten and warned to stop speaking in Jesus' name, Luke tells us, "Every day, in the temple and from house to house, they kept right on teaching and preaching Jesus as the Christ" (Acts 5:42). The apostles were more concerned with the healthy discipleship of new believers than with their own physical well-being.

Paul developed a similar pattern of public and small group training. Using the facility at the school of Tyrannus, Paul daily trained disciples (Acts 19:10). Yet Paul also trained leaders in their homes: "I did not

---

30   The roles of outside and inside teachers will be discussed later in this chapter as well. Initially an outside teacher will train the inside network teachers. Before long, an inside teacher arises from other inside teachers as the teacher who trains the inside teachers.

shrink from declaring to you anything that was profitable, and teaching you publicly and from house to house" (Acts 20:20).

Practically speaking, a training center isn't required. Disciples can be trained in smaller groups in homes or other available places. Where security is an issue, this may be the only option.

Gifted Equippers Arise

Many laypeople won't feel capable implementing leadership training. The good news is that not everyone has to be unusually gifted to equip other leaders![31]

> And He gave some as apostles, and some as prophets, and some as evangelists, and some as pastors and teachers, for the equipping of the saints for the work of service, to the building up of the body of Christ; until we all attain to the unity of the faith, and of the knowledge of the Son of God, to a mature man, to the measure of the stature which belongs to the fullness of Christ (Eph. 4:11–13).

Just as pastors equip church members to do their priestly tasks, some believers are gifted to equip leaders. It's important to identify believers, even from within young churches, whose character is becoming more Christ-like and who have gifts of leadership and teaching.

A group of churches needed someone to train teachers within its growing network. As the field workers struggled in prayer for many months, they considered who could be brought in from among their colleagues to accomplish this important task. Finally, the field workers realized the answer was right before them. A local believer named Jon could do the job if the training approach were simplified. Because of Jon, we've learned to look within, rather than outside, the local church.

Jon has become a model trainer of other teachers within the larger network of churches. His love for Christ is evident in his lifestyle. His teaching is simple and easy to understand and imitate. Other network leaders trust him, rather than feeling threatened by him. Jon is a teacher, and we've learned to utilize him to train other teachers.

---

31   At first, a trusted partner with advanced theological training (i.e. the pastor of an established church) might develop and teach leadership training lessons. However, the goal is for someone from the movement to be trained and, once he has proven faithful, become the trainer of the network teachers.

Maximize People's Priority Giftedness

As churches develop, the Spirit gifts certain believers to equip others. These often take the roles of apostles, prophets, evangelists, pastors and teachers. It's important to maximize the giftedness of these believers. Although some will have other areas of giftedness, it's important to prioritize these strategic areas because these gifts edify the church and equip others to fulfill their ministries.

The apostles of Acts could have themselves ministered to the Hellenistic Jewish widows, but instead they appointed seven servants for that task. Why? So, the apostles could focus on prayer and the ministry of the Word (Acts 6:4).[32] They emphasized advancing the spread of the gospel—preaching Jesus as the Christ—and discipling believers. The point seems to be that fewer people are gifted as apostles and teachers, so those with these gifts should assume these roles and allow others to apply their different gifts to edify the body of Christ in other ways.

The above servants in Acts 6 are good examples to those who aren't chosen as overseers. They were of good reputation, as well as full of the Spirit and wisdom. The filling of the Spirit is intrinsically related to proclaiming God's word and sharing the gospel in Acts. Stephen, Phillip and the others continued proclaiming the gospel, even while they fulfilled the other tasks for which they were specifically gifted. (Acts 6:8–10; 7:52; 8:4–5, 25–35).

Outside and Inside Teachers

Throughout the church planting process, the outside field-worker implements the plan and trains other partners to do so. When the first believers come to faith, the outside teacher trains the new believers to implement the plan as it has been modeled it for them. Ideally, the outside teacher would then transition to a coaching role, discipling and giving guidance to local believers.

Before long, Lord willing, inside teachers will emerge from the new churches. These inside teachers must be discipled and trained to dis-

---

32   All spiritual gifts are vital to edify and equip the church. Even so, priority is placed on the gifts of teaching and proclaiming the word of God. See also Paul's discussion of this issue where he prioritizes the gift of prophecy over other gifts (1 Cor. 14:1, 39–40).

pense deeper teaching to other leaders of groups/churches in their areas. The best teachers reproduce themselves (2 Tim. 2:2).

The Antioch church is a good example of multiplying local teachers. Initially, Antioch had five prophets and teachers (Acts 13:1). After the first missionary journey, the number of teachers had multiplied: "But Paul and Barnabas stayed in Antioch, teaching and preaching with many others also, the word of the Lord" (Acts 15:35).

Who are the Teachers?

In emerging church networks, we look for overseers, who are gifted to teach the leaders from the other churches as well. Even before overseers are appointed, we begin to identify potential teachers with these four characteristics: First, they must have good character. Second, they must believe the Bible and be able to communicate it within their context. Third, others pay attention to and implement what they teach. Fourth, they must have a good relationship with those who started the network.

Where are the Teachers?

How can these teachers be identified? Outside field-workers often don't have the access to find gifted teachers among generational churches. Generally, it's those who start and facilitate church networks who can help identify believers with the character and ability to serve as network teachers.

Utilizing Network Teachers

The greatest need of church leaders, after receiving foundational studies, is Bible knowledge.

Identifying and training network teachers is the best way we've found to hold church leaders accountable and impart deeper teaching to them, while having accountability for continued church planting. Our team implements a system which gathers and trains network teachers monthly. The network teachers then meet bi-weekly with the other overseers of their church network to teach the new lesson, while celebrating both deeper spiritual growth and the broader spread of the gospel. Sample templates for leadership development, emphasizing both going farther and growing deeper, are in Appendices C and D. First topics to consider for training leaders include God, The Gospel, Church, Overview of the Bible (Grand Narrative of the Scripture), Spiritual Victory (Overcoming Temptation), Priesthood of the Believer, Spiritual Disciplines and Church Leader Tasks and Qualifications.

Other topics might include New Testament, Old Testament, Worship, Evangelism, the Holy Spirit, Stewardship, Spiritual Gifts and Family Relationships.[33] In addition to systematic doctrinal and topical themes, entire portions and books of the Bible should be studied. Again, the greatest need of movement leaders, after receiving foundational studies, is Bible knowledge. Often, we'll study the entire New Testament book by book.

The key is to dispense all material in manageable portions. Through an ongoing system of generational accountability, leaders have the opportunity to study, apply and lead their churches through an informal, practical theological education.

---

33   Most of the topics in this section can be taught well using the sample format in Appendix B. More complicated lessons—like the ones about God, New Testament, Old Testament and How to Study the Bible—must be taught in a longer format. Sometimes these are best taught in all-day, big-group training events.

Part Five: Discipleship Re-en-Act-ment

15. Greater Works Guide

It's time to think through how you might specifically abide in Christ and build your *Plan A* plan. As previously mentioned, John's Upper Room Discourse provides a framework for glorifying God by abiding in Christ to fulfill the Great Commission.

Our customized version of the Greater Works Guide is in Appendix A. It is often called "Big One", because we draw it on a diagram shaped like a large number "1". You might benefit from looking at our plan as a reference, as you form you own plan.

Abiding In Christ

We'll never experience the greater works of Christ apart from abiding in Christ (John 15:1–8).[34] Thankfully, in the Upper Room Jesus taught His followers how to abide in Him.

---

34 Abiding in Christ and living in the Spirit are two ways of describing the same reality.

Two Prerequisites

Humility

Read John 15:4–5, 14:18–20 and 17:20–23. Abiding in Christ (oneness with Christ) is the key to bearing fruit and experiencing Jesus' promise that we'll do greater works than He did.

- Read John 13:1–9. Jesus is our model for humility.
- After reading, answer the following questions:
- According to verse 3, what do we learn about Jesus?
- In verses 4–5, whose feet did Jesus wash?
- Did Jesus wash Judas Iscariot's feet?
- To what degree did Jesus exemplify humility to His disciples?
- According to verses 8–9, when Peter humbled himself, what change did he have to make based on the Lord's word?

How can we follow Jesus' example and humble ourselves?

Jesus: First and Only

In order for us to abide in Christ, we must humble ourselves toward the lost, as well as every other believer, new and mature, as they perform the works of Christ. Humility demands we have the attitude that "It doesn't matter which of us succeeds, as long as the gospel succeeds." Each of us must rejoice if any of those we lead to faith bears greater fruit than we do, because Christ's kingdom is expanding, and He is being glorified!

"Yes, Lord"

Humility requires obedience to Jesus and His word. Peter was thinking about the tradition of servants washing their master's feet when he told Jesus, "Never shall you wash my feet" (John 13:8). He meant well, but his response showed the pride in his heart. The only appropriate response to Christ is "Yes, Lord."

Humility demands we always do what Christ says, regardless of tradition. Jesus challenged the Pharisees in this regard when He asked, "Why do you yourselves transgress the commandment of God for the sake of your tradition?" Are there changes you must make to humbly obey Christ's word?

Willingness to Die (Surrendered)

Read John 15:13–16; 16:2. What requirements from each of these passages are related to abiding in Christ and accomplishing the greater works Christ promised? If we want to produce much fruit, we must die to our own desires and be ready to lay down our lives.

3 Conditions for Abiding in Christ

John 15:1–8 summarizes three conditions for us to bear much fruit in our work. These are also conditions the Bible sets for abiding in Christ.

Christ's Walk (Prayer)

- Study John 14:13–14; 15:7–8, 16; 16:23–24. What do these verses teach about abiding in Christ through prayer?

Summary: Jesus promised that if we would abide in Him and His Word abides in us, we can ask whatever we wish, and the Father will give it to us. This is so God will be glorified. God wants to answer our prayers. Jesus Himself prayed regularly as a part of His daily walk. The church gathered together constantly to pray as a group.

Application: Evaluate your prayer life:

- Are you praying regularly in accordance with the Scriptures?

- What adjustments should you make to walk with Christ in prayer?

Christ's Word

Study John 14:15, 21–24; 15:10. What do these verses teach about Jesus' words (commands)?

Summary: If we truly love Jesus, we obey His commands.

Application: What adjustments do you need to make to abide in Christ according to His Word? Are there any commands you presently are not obeying? The following six responses to God's Word might be helpful to make an action plan: hear, study, meditate, memorize, do and teach.

Christ's Works

- Study John 14:10–12; 17:4. Doing the works of Christ is foundational to abiding in Christ.

Application: Be bold in evangelism. Abide in Christ, and share the gospel regularly. For those who seem open to the message, we follow up. For those who don't seem open, we either persist in sharing or move on.

Follow-Up with New Believers

Baptism is the first step of obedience for a new believer. Explain the meaning of baptism from Romans 6:4 and note that the Lord has commanded every follower of Christ to be baptized. Also, be sure to clarify that baptism is only for Christians, so we should seek to ascertain as best as we can that this profession of faith is genuine. It should also accompany a biblical understanding of repentance and lifelong discipleship.

After baptism, new believers should be taught to learn Scripture; we've benefitted from memorizing 1 Peter 1:14–16. We'll particularly emphasize the importance of breaking from idolatry (inherent in many indigenous belief systems) and sexual immorality.

Instill Multiplying Discipleship

Our initial follow-up lessons focus on the new believer's relationship with God. We also prepare them to immediately invite their family, friends and acquaintances to follow Jesus with them.

We first teach new believers to make lists of their family, friends and acquaintances who need the Lord, then under the leading of the Holy Spirit to identify the first five people with whom they will share the gospel. We then train new believers in a simple, reproducible gospel presentation and invitation, preferably the presentation that led them to faith.

As God begins saving the new believer's relational network, it becomes necessary for these new believers to either join existing churches or begin one of their own. Be ready to shepherd the new believer(s) to gather those coming to faith to become a church. This may or may not happen quickly. The goal is not rapid growth, but lasting multiplication.

This is why casting a vision for church planting is so important. Gatherings don't need to be complex; they simply need to reflect Scripture. Teach them about baptism and the Lord's Supper. Teach them how to pray and study the Bible. Teach them to hold one another accountable, and to sing Christ-centered hymns that fit their context. Of course, immediately teach them the importance of evangelizing so that the new church might soon multiply. Guide them to immediately become a church, with the goal of becoming a strong church.

Equip Churches and Leaders

As multiple churches develop, on-the-job training must be provided for church leaders and the leaders of their networks. This is best done informally and locally as much as possible. Using simple and reproducible leadership training materials is essential for church and network leaders to grow.

If leadership training is done primarily by outsiders—particularly outsiders with advanced education—local leadership development will bottleneck, resulting in a shortage of new leaders, and discipleship may suffer.

The goal in all this is not to communicate adherence to a specific method. Instead, we want to uphold grace-based obedience that's rooted in Christian doctrine and practice.

According to Zane Pratt,

> Grace-based obedience is explicitly theological. What we do is based on the truth of what we know. We cannot substitute obedience-based discipleship for information-based discipleship. We must teach both, with the theological truth of the New Testament as the foundation for the way we subsequently live.

> This is the obedience of faith. We obey because we trust Jesus to rule our lives wisely, even when He asks us to do things that go against the wisdom of this world.

> This is grace-based obedience. We do not obey in order to become right with God. We obey because He has graciously made us right with Himself, purely by grace, through the infinite cost of the sacrifice of His Son.

> We obey because we love Him. All fallen sinners like us have a tendency to turn obedience into the grounds of our relationship with God, even as believers. We must be very careful to guard against that, especially with new believers. We must present the commands of Scripture always on the clear foundations of theological truth, faith, grace and love.[35]

---

35   These guidelines for grace-based obedience were contributed by Zane Pratt, an experienced practitioner, regional leader, and now Vice President of Global Training at the IMB, SBC.

Developing a Greater Works Plan

Who are you trying to reach and disciple?

Greater Works Guide (Appendix A) is the plan we derived to disciple our Muslim people group. Understanding the Muslim mindset, we chose lessons from the Bible that spoke to their worldview. More importantly, we chose lessons that would give them an opportunity to respond to the gospel, follow Christ as new believers and multiply.

If the people you're trying to reach are religious (particularly Muslim, Catholic or traditional Christian groups), the basic approach used in Greater Works Guide may not need many adjustments to be effective. However, if you're trying to reach people who have a secular or less-defined religious system, you might choose different lessons within the same or a similar framework.

How Will You Share the Gospel?

You will need to adopt, devise or revise a way to communicate the gospel and woo the person to Christ. How will you share the gospel to filter for openness?

Also, get your baptism strategy ready. When the Spirit draws someone to faith, you must be prepared to do the second task of the Great Commission according to the Acts pattern.

How Will You Follow Up Those Who Are Open to the Gospel?

When the gospel is shared, some people will be open but will not respond in faith during the initial meeting. You must have a plan for following up such persons. I suggest having a set of five or six lessons for those who are interested. Remember to include accountability for those open to the gospel, beginning with the first follow-up visit. They should be immediately sharing what they are learning with others.

We're finding that most people profess faith during the first or second follow-up visit, sometimes the third one. If they haven't professed faith by the third follow-up visit, they will not likely receive Christ anytime soon. If people haven't responded to Christ by the end of the short set of follow-up lessons, then we move on to others.

Content

How will you follow up with those who are open to the gospel, but haven't yet professed faith? For working with Muslims, we chose the Old Testament sacrifice stories: Adam and Eve, Cain and Abel, Noah, Abraham and Moses. These lessons show the demand for sacrifice for the forgiveness of sin and point to Christ's atoning sacrifice as their fulfillment. With these stories, we share the gospel each time we meet, until the open person(s) professes faith or the lesson set is complete.

Process

Having a simple discipleship process that includes accountability with support, interactive Bible study, training and goals makes aggressive obedience and multiplication more likely. Mutual accountability was certainly part of the early discipleship and church process (see Hebrews 10:24-25). Unfortunately, we don't know the exact process used by the apostles. However, applying an adapted version of the 3/3 process of T4T[36] has enabled us to establish a reproducing pattern of discipleship.

Beginning with the first follow-up visit, we implement three simple objectives. First, we celebrate stewardship by accountability with support. Next, we study the Bible together and then pray for the person(s) in Jesus' name. In so doing, we set a pattern for what we'll do each time we meet together. In addition, we model a Bible study approach they can implement with others, even when we're not in attendance.

Once people believe the gospel and are gathering to become churches, we insert additional elements, forming a well-developed pattern for church meetings. We further develop the pattern for equipping emerging church leaders. But, especially at first, keep it simple!

How Will You Follow Up Those Who Receive the Gospel?

What are the first lessons you'll teach new believers? These are the lessons most important to ground them spiritually and prepare them to gather a group.

---

36   Steve Smith, T4T: Discipleship Re-Revolution (Monument, Colorado: WIGTake Resources, 2011).

We start with lessons about baptism, the results of repentance (emphasizing breaking from idolatry and sexual immorality) and abiding in Christ. After this, we teach three lessons to prepare them to gather and reach their oikos (family, friends and other acquaintances). These are the formal lessons, and we fill in the gaps with whatever else they need. Soon they'll have formal lessons about those things as well.

How will You Guide New Believers to be a Church of Mature Believers?

Content

After the initial lessons, new believers will study the ten stages (20 lessons) for becoming mature believers. These lessons are described in Appendix A. You might choose to use different lessons.[37] Decide which New Testament book will be studied once the early church lessons have been completed.[38]

Process

As previously stated, we adapt the 3/3 process of T4T[39] to form our full worship pattern. The pattern we use includes the following elements:

1. Celebrate stewardship
   a. Confession of faith
   b. Our vision: "The gospel for every person and a church in every community."
   c. Accountability with support
   d. Mutual concern and prayer
2. Gain life through the word and worship
   a. Indigenous songs and choruses

---

37   Remember that once a meeting format and study process is set, a lesson might be as simple as a passage, memory verse and perhaps a summary of the conclusion.

38   Most of our churches study passage by passage through Mark, Acts, Ephesians and then other NT books and passages.

39   Steve Smith, T4T.

    b. Interactive Bible study[40]
       i. What is this passage about?
      ii. What do we learn about God from this passage?
     iii. What is the most interesting part of this passage to you?
     iv. Why is this passage still relevant?
      v. What must we do to obey this passage?
     vi. With whom (three people) will you share this passage?
3. Sending
    a. Training (Include reviewing the lesson and memorizing a verse together).
    b. Goals
       i. To whom will each person teach the lesson (three people)?
      ii. With whom will each person share the gospel (three people)?
    c. Commissioning prayer

How Will You Equip Leaders?

Think about the leadership development pattern mentioned in this chapter. How will you identify and train network teachers? Which lessons are top priority? Will your system facilitate both going (outreach) and growing (deeper discipleship)? Notice the leadership development templates in Appendices B and C. These are organized in three parts: Celebrate the Work, Study the Word and Send the Workers.

---

40   These first two questions frame the passage in its context and theological intent. The third examines the parts of the passage. The fourth and fifth deal with relevance and application. The last focuses the disciple on teaching others. Realizing that new believers don't yet understand the larger context of Scripture, we add a learning summary—usually in the form of an acronym—to guide the conclusion and application of their first 20 lessons at the church level, as described in Appendix A.

16. Keys for Effective Training

We've Lost Our Keys

Training is a lost art. Let's consider several deficiencies in training that often hinder the third task of the Great Commission.

We teach but don't train.

How many sermons and lessons have been delivered about the need to witness? Yet how many Christians, other than pastoral staff, witness consistently and effectively? We blame it on apathy, and for many that is the right diagnosis. However, I suspect sincere believers would witness more if they were trained to do so.

When we do train people to witness, only rarely is it the new converts who are receiving the training. But new converts should be trained to reach their family members, friends and acquaintances. A new believer will likely never have a more opportune moment to share his faith with others than right after he first believes.

Our methods are too complicated.

Most of our current methodology makes the challenge of training insurmountable. Too much of what we do is geared toward an elite class of Christian worker, either clergy or laity. The complexity of our methods and materials limits implementation.

New believers often watch with admiration and a desire to get involved. After all, training should improve the ability and confidence of the trainee to do what's asked of him.

We don't hold new believers accountable to obey what they have been taught. Somewhere in the process of attempting to make disciples, we've gotten away from the norm of holding one another accountable. Jesus held His disciples accountable.

In Luke 9:1–9 Jesus equipped the disciples, gave them authority and sent them out. But look at Luke 9: 10: "When the apostles returned, they gave an account to Him of all that they had done." Similarly, Mark 6:30 states, "The apostles gathered together with Jesus; and they reported to Him all that they had done and taught." The author of Hebrews reminds the church of the need to hold one another accountable through the regular gathering (Heb. 10:25). It appears the first-century church understood the importance of not only giving assignments but encouraging one another to implement them.

Model, Assist, Watch, Let Them Do It[41]

Our goal in all this is to cultivate local leadership. The apostles rarely stayed in one area very long. When they left, however, church networks were functioning, led primarily by locals. The apostle Paul, for instance, would entrust occasionally visit or write a letter to give instruction, but local leaders led local churches and church networks.

It's important not to model for too long. Moving quickly from modeling to assisting allows new believers to "own" their ministry. By modeling new tasks and then transferring ownership to the new believer, the transition to the assist phase has begun. One can assist as long as necessary to encourage the new believer; what's important is that new believers have a stake in ministry.

While transitioning through the training process, we increasingly "commend" the developing leaders to the Lord, rather than to ourselves. This was the Acts pattern (Acts 14:23; 20:32).

The most frequent problem preventing the transfer of leadership is taking too long. The key is to model a skill once or twice, then require the trainee to do the skill from that point forward. The trainer can assist the trainee as long as genuinely needed, but multiplication depends on making the transition from modeling to assisting.

The new believer will rarely feel qualified to perform the task after seeing it done one or two times. Perhaps they can do it with some assistance. Of course, the trainer could do it better than the trainee at this early point, but it's vital for the trainer to encourage the trainee to do the task, even if the trainee struggles. With time, the trainee becomes more than competent, and the trainer is free to start new work in a different area.

---

41   David Garrison originally labeled this "Model, Assist, Watch and Leave" in Church Planting Movements, (WIGTake Resources, Monument, Colorado, 2004), p. 257.

This quick transition works. Ongoing leadership training allows the outsider, or a trained insider, to influence the movement without controlling it. Sometimes, however, during the process, the trainer must slow down to ensure that the process stays true to Scripture.

"Yes, You Can. You Have Help"

"I'll Help You"

New believers generally don't feel competent right away. Their natural tendency is to defer to the one who led them to faith. But it's very important for new believers to do for others what was done for them. If you're willing to do things for them, they'll welcome your involvement. In the process, however, they'll become your dependent, rather than your partner.

"Christ Will Help You"

This is the culminating promise of the Great Commission: "I am with you always, even to the end of the age" (Matt. 28:20). Jesus echoed this promise in the Upper Room: "I will ask the Father, and He will give you another Helper, that He may be with you forever" (John 14:16). Christ's presence in the new believer's life, via the indwelling Holy Spirit, offers help to the new believer-priest. Working with Christ, they learn to know Christ and depend on Him as He works. The believers gain an unforgettable testimony of what Christ does through them.

When new believers doubt, try encouraging them by saying, "You can do this. You have help." By doing so, you transfer ownership to them, making them an equal partner-priest. You've gone from modeling to assisting, and in the process, you're commend them to the Lord and not primarily to yourself.

You'll hold one another accountable as you meet regularly to discuss both personal spiritual growth and the establishing of new groups. This is how you help them become partners instead of sympathizers. Meetings will be frequent in the initial, critical stages, but they'll become more sporadic in following stages. Each new believer should meet with at least one other believer for growth and accountability, especially while the new believer is developing a group in a different area.

Give Attention to the Obedient Disciples

Discipleship demands obedience. The believer-priest should give primary attention to those who are doing Christ's works, instead of those who are merely showing up. Jesus Himself set this precedent. He prioritized the doers of the word over any other natural relationship (Mark 3:33–35). Those who disciple like Jesus prioritize obedient believers. Discipling should continue as long as the believer obeys what's being taught. If he or she doesn't obey the Word, then there's no obligation to continue the process.

Training at Their Level

For more than 13 years as a pastor and professor, I *taught* people to obey God's Word. For the past eight years I have invested in *training* people to obey God's Word. What follows are some key differences between teaching and training.

Train Them Where They Are

Whether or not people obey often depends on how they are trained, not what they are taught. On the field, we use what we call "straw mat" training instead of "podium training." The concept is simply—you train people where they're most comfortable, instead of where you are most comfortable.

Train for the Future

Training must occur at a level appropriate for beginners, rather than expecting the new believers to have already attained the same maturity as the trainer. In our context, that means we talk more slowly, repeat key concepts and keep content compact and transferable. Stay as basic as possible, without diluting biblical truth. Put simply, train for the educational level of those whom the new believers will, Lord willing, one day train themselves. It's wise to train according to what level the next two generations will understand.

Train Them Informally

Another important key is informality. Discipling can be done by everyday people in everyday places as they live their everyday lives. This lack of structure helps the gospel and the church develop organically, rather than into compartmentalized sections of "sacred" and "secular."

If everyday life consists of wearing blue jeans and T-shirts, do training that way. If you're training business people, train them according to their context.

Train in informal places as well. One believer discovered that when training was done in established church buildings, only a small percentage of participants implemented Great Commission principles. However, when the same kind of training was done in informal contexts like coffee shops or homes, more believers responded faithfully. It's important to train people where they are.

Training to Succeed

Train Over and Over Again

Training only succeeds when trainees "get it" and "do it." If at first they don't succeed, train them again and provide support if necessary. Even when people have proven they can do what they've been trained to do, it's important to review the principles. The following verses from 2 Peter reinforce this point.

Therefore, I will always be ready to remind you of these things, even though you already know them, and have been established in the truth which is present with you. I consider it right, as long as I am in this earthly dwelling, to stir you up by way of reminder, knowing that the laying aside of my earthly dwelling is imminent, as also our Lord Jesus Christ has made clear to me. And I will also be diligent that at any time after my departure you will be able to call these things to mind (2 Peter 1:12–15).

These verses show the importance of reviewing important concepts over and over until they become second nature to the person receiving them. Sometimes, the trainer will feel frustrated at repeatedly re-hashing the same principles, but the reward of seeing future fruit makes it worthwhile. So long as they're making progress, train them.

See Their Potential

I love seeing God do through others what they never dreamed was possible. Picture undereducated farmers and fishermen who've come to faith and started churches. Early in their journey of faith, they truly thought they couldn't do such a thing. However, by training them and expecting them to do the Great Commission, the Holy Spirit has done it through them.

Don't evaluate the new believer's potential by how he performs skills in your presence. In almost every situation, he'll perform better in his own setting among people he already knows well.

Months after training starts, we often laugh together as we consider where the new believers were then and how far they've come. Who—besides the Holy Spirit—would have thought simple believer-priests like us would become teachers and church leaders?

Who'd have thought Andy would start a generational church that led to other churches? Andy was "street smart" but not "book smart." He wasn't a good communicator. On top of that, he was quirky and a bit socially awkward. Even so Andy loved Jesus and boldly followed Him.

When we trained Andy, he only could recount bits and pieces during the training sessions. But with the Lord's help Andy took the bits he retained and applied them. Andy reached his family first and formed a house church. He's also reached others who have started house churches, multiplying to the sixth generation.

Friends and I have commented that the quality of believers in these churches often exceeds those in other networks. It's a good thing we didn't judge his potential based on appearance.

17. *Plan A* for Your Local Church

Obedience to the Great Commission requires not only local evangelism, but also a vision for the world's other people groups. Depending on where you live, these people groups might be located in a nearby neighborhood or city. It's more likely, however, that most of the world's people groups are in distant lands.

Evangelistic churches aren't necessarily Great Commission churches. Many churches aren't reaching their Jerusalem (local people similar to themselves). Others aren't reaching their Judea (people in the larger local area similar to themselves. Most churches aren't reaching their "Samaria" (people in the general area and beyond, of different ethnicity or characteristics such as socio-economic status, class differences, etc.). Still fewer churches are involved in cross-cultural missions to "the ends of the earth."

"Come-Mission" Churches Can Become "Go-Mission Churches" Churches must follow the biblical pattern of praying, giving and sending for each range of their responsibility: Jerusalem, Judea, Samaria and the ends of the earth. Every church, large or small, can become a Great Commission church.

Much has been written about how churches can reach their local areas. But our local strategies should be evaluated in light of Great Commission principles. Enhancing church programs will likely attract people. However, training each church member to evangelize will involve more believers in evangelism, not just the pastor and staff.

Many churches have a strategy for international missions. They often pray for international missionaries and give to mission organizations. Direct involvement is also increasingly common, and many churches are sending people for both short-term and career assignments. More and more churches also are awakening to the possibility of impacting an unreached people group through prayer and long-term engagement.

Very few churches, however, try to reach their Samaria the same way. Churches are often involved in social programs directed toward Samaritans, but rarely have a strategy to multiply in neighboring areas among other ethnic groups.

Discipling Samaria from Your Local Church

Churches generally reach those who are like them, but traditional methods haven't been as effective in reaching Samaria. That's because reaching our Samaria requires a Great Commission strategy. Implementation of this strategy doesn't need to be very complicated. There are reasons why the Samaritans don't come to church. However, if they are reached and trained to start Samaritan churches in their homes, many will catch the vision and thousands of Samaritans will come into the kingdom.

In the same way that your church aims to disciple its Samaria, it can send apostolic teams farther, discipling people groups to the ends of the earth. In fact, many churches are proclaiming the gospel around the world as they send teams prepared not only to lead people to faith and baptize them, but also to group them in multiplying churches.

Hopefully, we now see more clearly the church planting pattern in Acts. implementing and training toward a more biblical—and therefore more effective—method. With increasing frequency, generational churches and church networks are being planted and are becoming spiritually mature.

Stay the Course

This book has emphasized the concept of "going." Equally important are those who send, and those who go and stay—especially as difficulties arise.

After all, movements rarely start immediately, even when we are implementing an effective method. The Lord often molds and shapes the Christian workers and their strategies before breakthroughs occur. For example, we once engaged an unreached people group for eight months before seeing our first new believer. By God's grace, hundreds have come to faith since. It's not unusual for movements to start slowly.

We've faced intense persecution and seeming insurmountable obstacles at times, but the Lord gave timely answers to our prayers. The answers often came later than we anticipated. However, we kept working while waiting for God to act. Had we given up at any point, we might have missed the blessings that have come through endurance.

Celebrate

Finally, in the midst of all the difficulties, remember to celebrate. In the Lord's kindness, you're being given a front row seat to the fulfillment not only of the Great Commission, but also of God's promise to Abram in Genesis 12 and His vision to John in Revelation 7.

Celebrate *obedience*. Each time a team member does what he or she has been taught, celebrate. Obedience is gracious, Holy Spirit-wrought fruit. Celebrate, then send them out with the next assignment.

Celebrate *fruitfulness*. Each time a new believer professes faith and is baptized, celebrate. Celebrate also the steady planting of each new group, praying for it to one day become a church.

Celebrate *generational growth*. When believers lead others to faith and baptize them, celebrate. And when those believers repeat the process, celebrate. Celebrate whenever a new group is planted, and whenever a member of that group plants yet another new group.

Finally, celebrate that the Holy Spirit is working the Son's plan through us, His priests. God is receiving the glory He deserves because of the gospel. As you celebrate, join the new song in heaven:

Worthy are You to take the book and to break its seals; for You were slain, and purchased for God with Your blood men from every tribe and tongue and people and nation. You have made them to be a kingdom and priests to our God; and they will reign upon the earth. (Rev. 5:9–10)

Appendices

Appendix A:
Greater Works Guide Plan

This implements the principles of *Plan A*. It is sometimes referred to as the "Big One" because our summary diagram is shaped like a big "1".

I.   **Abiding in Christ** (John 13-17):
      A. **Walk with Christ in prayer**
      B. **Obey Christ's word**
      C. **Do Christ's works**
II.   **Bold Evangelism** (Any-3)[42] and Follow-Up

Any-3 **Evangelism Approach (John 4:1-42)**

      A. **Get Connected** (build rapport through small talk)
          1. Ask "How are you?" questions
          2. Ask "Who are you?" questions
      B. **Get to a God Conversation** (transition to spiritual matters)
          1. Pray for an open door.
          2. If a door doesn't open immediately, ask: "Do you have any particular spiritual beliefs?"
          3. Guide the conversation along these lines: "Almost all religions are the same, aren't they?" "The point of religion is to try to be good enough to please God, so God will receive us. Nearly all religions are concerned with doing good things to offset our sins, but we never get our sins paid off." "We are all

---

42   Any-3 has been applied effectively world-wide in Muslim contexts and has been adapted effectively in various non-Muslim contexts.

frustrated, aren't we? We try our best to please God, but fail (sin) continually, leaving us frustrated."

"We are all sinners, aren't we?" "Because we sin every day, our sin debt gets larger instead of smaller, doesn't it?"

    C.   **Get to Lostness** (ask about their religious experience)
1. What are you doing to pay off your sins? (Let them talk about three to five things they are doing to get their sins forgiven, then ask the following questions.)
2. Are your sins paid off (forgiven) yet?
3. When will they be paid off (forgiven)?
4. In eternity, will your sins be forgiven?

    D.   **Get to the Gospel** (tell "The First and Last Sacrifice Story")
1. Say, "What I believe is different. My sins are forgiven because God Himself made a way for our sins to be forgiven."
2. Tell the story (Appendix B)

    E.   **Get to a Decision**
1. If they are not open to the gospel, move on for now.
2. If they are open to the gospel:
    a. Use the following questions to invite them to receive Christ:
      1). "Does this make sense?"
      2). "Have you ever heard this before?"
      3). "Do you believe this?"
    b. If they seem ready, read and discuss Romans 10:9-10 with them and invite them to receive Christ.
3. If open, but not ready to profess faith, briefly tell them another relevant gospel story, or invite them to discuss another story later the same week.

Follow-Up Process for Open People

Share the gospel, then follow up those who are open:

    A.   **Simplified 3/3 Process:**
1. Ask if they shared the previous story, and what happened.
2. Study a new lesson (story) using the six questions below
3. Pray for them in Jesus' name.

    B.   **Gospel Stories** (select a series of stories appropriate to your context)

6 Questions for Interactive Study:

1. Can you retell the story (with help of the group leader as needed)?
2. What do we learn about God in this story?
3. What is the most interesting part of the story to you?
4. Why is the story still relevant today?
5. What do we have to do to obey the intention of this story?
6. With whom (3-5 people) will you share this story?

Note: Whenever an open person(s) professes faith, take them immediately through the steps below in "Follow-Up Process for New Converts." Should the profession of faith come before all the gospel stories have been studied, have the new believer(s) complete the "Follow-Up Process for New Converts," then master the remaining gospel stories. This will equip them to reach and group their oikos.

III.   **Instill Multiplying Discipleship**

Follow-Up Process for New Believers (Short-Term Discipleship)

A. **Baptism** (taught immediately after profession of faith)
1. Teach "1, 2, 3 Obey the Great Commission."
   a. One Command (disciple All ethnic groups)
   b. Two Assurances (Christ's Authority and Accompaniment)
   c. Three Tasks: Going, Baptizing and Teaching
2. Discuss the meaning of baptism in Romans 4 (the death/resurrection of Jesus Christ, as the believer surrenders to His Lordship)
3. Tell the Ethiopian Official Story (Acts 8:25-40) and **Baptize** the believer(s).
B. **Results of Repentance** (study Acts 19:13-20)
1. Emphasize stopping immoral sexual behavior
2. Memorize 1 Pet. 1:14-16
C. **Abiding in Christ** (study John 15:1-8)
1. Learn these three keys to abiding in Christ:
   a. Pray Constantly,
   b. Obey His Commandments
   c. Do His Works
2. Memorize John 15:5

    D. **Cornelius Story**
        1. Study Acts 10:1-48
        2. Memorize 2 Timothy 2:2
        3. Make Lists of lost Family, Friends and Acquaintances.
    E. *Any-3*: Train to use the First and Last Sacrifice Story to share the gospel
    F. **Philippian Jailer Story**
        1. Study Acts 16:22-34
        2. Teach three factors for reaching family, friends and acquaintances:
           a. The new believer's *changed life*
           b. The **power** of Jesus Christ through prayer
           c. The **Gospel**
        3. Memorize Acts 16:31
        4. Pray with them from their Family, Friends and Acquaintances Lists
        5. Help the believer choose five from their lists with whom to use *Any-3* (Guide new believers to gather open people from their relational network for the "Follow-Up Process for Open People." As these "open" persons come to faith, the one leading them will repeat the process—guiding those new believers through "Follow-Up for New Believers.")

IV. **Develop Churches (Long-Term Discipleship)** When believers have completed the short-term discipleship lessons, they will then go through long-term lessons together that will guide them to become a church. Following are the distinct characteristics and lessons of long-term discipleship.

Full 3/3 Pattern, adapted

    A. **Profession of faith**
        1. "Jesus Christ is Lord, to the glory of God the Father" (Philippians 2:11b).
        2. "He wants all men to be saved and to come to the knowledge of the truth. For there is one God and one mediator between God and men, the man Christ Jesus, who gave Himself as a ransom for all men" (1 Tim. 2:4-6a).
    B. **Six Question Process of Bible Study** Lessons are directly from the Bible. If not in story form, focus attention on the text by replacing retelling with the question, "What is this text about?"

C. **Summary Lesson and Memory Verse**
   1. The group leader gives a brief lesson summary
   2. The group reads the memory verse aloud together seven times
   3. In groups of four people have each teach the lesson summary to the other three group members, then lead the group to read the verse together seven more times. This way each person experiences or teaches the summary five times and reads the verse 35 times.[43]
D. **Ten Stages of Growth** After completing the short-term discipleship lessons, the first 20 lessons for believers help groups become strong churches. These 20 lessons cover 10 stages of growth:
   1. Identification with the Death of Jesus Christ
   2. New Birth
   3. New Family (The Body of Christ)
   4. Communicating with God (Prayer)
   5. Spiritual Food (The Word of God)
   6. The Clothing of Followers of Jesus
   7. Stand Firm (Power over Dark Powers)
   8. Walk as a Follower of Jesus
   9. Developing Personal Characteristics as a Follower of Jesus
   10. Towards Maturity

V. **Long-Term Discipleship Lessons**[44]
A. **Identification with the Death of Jesus Christ**
   1. **The Lord's Supper**
      a. *Learning Goal:* Understand and observe the Lord's Supper
      b. *Study* Matthew 26:26-35 (using *Six Questions*)
      c. *Memory Verse:* Galatians 2:20
      d. *Application:*
         1). Like baptism, Jesus commanded the Lord's Supper as a symbol to remind each of His followers of His sacrifice for the forgiveness of sin.
         2). Each follower of Jesus who surrenders himself for baptism may partake in the Lord's Supper.

---

43   This approach was modified from Dan Lancaster's approach in the Follow Jesus Seminar.
44   Some of the long-term discipleship lessons (2A, 3A, 4A, 5A in particular) were adapted from or influenced by Dan Lancaster's Follow Jesus Seminar. Some of the other lessons were adapted from or influenced by Steve Smith's T4T.

3). Before partaking in the Lord's Supper, followers of Jesus must cleanse themselves by forgiving others and confessing their sins (1 Cor. 11:27).

4). The group should choose who leads the Lord's Supper.

5). Celebrate the Lord's Supper together.

2. **Facing Persecution**

a. *Learning Goal:* Overcome temptation

b. *Study* Acts 4:13-31 (using *Six Questions*)

c. *Memory Verse:* Luke 9:23

d. *Summary* (with hand motions)

1). Responding to those who persecute you:

2). Don't repay evil with evil

3). Share the gospel

4). Bless them

5). Pray for them

6). Help them

7). Love them

8). Forgive them

e. *Application* (daily):

1). Review Luke 9:23

2). Read Matt. 5:44 and pray for those who persecute you

3). Pray for one another, that you all may hold fast to your faith.

B. **New Birth**

1. **New Birth by the Holy Spirit**

a. *Learning Goal:* Experience New Birth in the Holy Spirit

b. *Study* John 3:1-18 (using *Six Questions*)

c. *Memory Verse:* 2 Corinthians 5:17

d. *Summary One:* Teach Trinity using fingers (0, 1, 3 in 1).

1). There is no other (0) Lord

2). Except the one (1) true God

3). Who is the Father, Son and Holy Spirit (3 in 1)

e. *Summary Two:* Four skits for four Holy Spirit commands:

1). Be filled with the Spirit

2). Walk in the Spirit

3). Don't grieve the Spirit

4). Don't quench the Spirit

f. Application:

1). The Holy Spirit is a person of the Godhead, just like Jesus (John 14:16). Father, Jesus and Holy Spirit are one God, so we are baptized in the name of the Father, Son and Holy Spirit (Matt. 28:19-20).

    2). The Holy Spirit dwells personally in believers (John 14:16-18).

  2. **Paul's Testimony**

    a. *Learning Goal:* Share your testimony regularly

    b. *Study* Acts 9:1-22 (using *Six Questions*)

    c. *Memory Verse:* Titus 3:5

    d. *Summary:* Four points to your testimony:

      1). Life before you received Jesus

      2). How you came to believe in Jesus

      3). Changes in your life since you surrendered to Jesus

      4). Do you want to know more?

    e. *Application:* Share your personal testimony with those who don't know Jesus.

C. New Family (The Body of Jesus Christ)

  1. **The Head of the Body (Obedience to Jesus Christ)**

    a. *Learning Goal:* Submission to Jesus Christ as Head of the Body

    b. *Study* Matthew 4:18-25 (using *Six Questions*)

    c. *Memory Verse:* Colossians 1:18

    d. *Summary:* Hand motions for obeying Christ's commands (based on the parable of the sons—Luke 15:11-31):

      1). Immediately

      2). Always

      3). Gladly

    e. *Application:* Each participant says: Yes Lord, I surrender my whole life to You. All my possessions, my talents, my future, I surrender to You today and forever.

  2. **The Functions of the Body**

    a. *Learning Goal:* Learn five church functions (with hand gestures)

    b. *Study* Acts 2:29-47 (using *Six Questions*)

    c. *Memory Verse:* 1 Corinthians 12:13a

    d. *Lesson Summary:* Covenant to be a "STRONG" church:

      1). Sole authority is the Bible

      2). Tasks of church all being done (5 Functions/2 Ordinances)

      3). Reproducing locally and throughout the World

      4). Ordinary believers leading, doing all duties and deciding together

        5). Not forsaking the assembly (meeting consistently)

        6). Governed locally (autonomous)

  e. *Application:* Five Functions of a Church (with hand motions)

        1). *Discipleship:* Form an open book with the palms of your hands.

        2). *Worship:* Raise hands as though worshipping.

        3). *Fellowship:* Join hands together as though shaking hands.

        4). *Ministry:* Choose hand-motion which communicates giving.

        5). *Evangelism:* Throw imaginary fishing net then draw it back in.

D. Communication with God (Prayer)

1. Building a Close Relationship with God through Prayer

  a. *Learning Goal:* Pray according to the Lord's Prayer

  b. *Study* Matthew 6:5-15 (using *Six Questions*)

  c. *Memory Verse:* Matthew 6:9-13

  d. *Summary:* Pray the five parts of the Lord's Prayer (Matt. 6:9-13)

  e. *Application:* Pray each phrase of the Lord's prayer together: Mention the two elements listed after each phrase, then each person prays according to the two elements before moving on to the next phrase of the Lord's Prayer

        1). "Our Father, who is in Heaven, holy is Your Name"— **Worship** and **Submit**

        2). "Your Kingdom come and Your will be done"—**His Kingdom** and **Will**

        3). "Give us this day our daily bread"—**Request** and **Beseech** (more intense)

        4). "Forgive us our debts as we forgive our debtors"— **Confess** and **Forgive**

        5). "Lead us not into temptation, but deliver us from evil"— **Leadership** and **Deliverance**

2. Building a Close Relationship with God through Prayer

  a. *Learning Goal:* Practice thanksgiving daily

  b. *Study* Matthew 7:7-11 (using *Six Questions*)

  c. *Memory Verse:* 1 Thessalonians 5:16-18

  d. *Summary:* Jesus' Cell Phone Number (John 14:14)

  e. *Application:* Commune with God in praise and intercession

E. **Spiritual Food (The Word of God)**
  1. **Building a Close Relationship with God through His Word**
    a. *Learning Goal:* Explore at least one passage each day from the Bible:
      1). What is the passage about?
      2). What must I do about what I have read?
      3). Who can I help with what I learned from this passage?
    b. *Study* Luke 24:36-45 (using *Six Questions*)
    c. *Memory Verse:* 1 Peter 2:2
    d. *Summary:* Using five fingers learn five responses to God's Word which lead to obedience (Hear, Meditate, Study, Memorize and Teach it to others)
    e. *Application:* Commit to explore at least one chapter each day from the Bible, beginning with Matthew:
      1). Pray that the Holy Spirit will teach you through His Word
      2). Read the chapter (or meditate on the memory verse)
      3). Answer the questions above for this chapter
      4). Meditate on what the Holy Spirit reveals
  2. **Visit with God (Quiet Time)**
    a. *Learning Goal:* Spend 30+ minutes a day with God
    b. *Study* Luke 10:38-42 (using *Six Questions*)
    c. *Memory Verse:* John 15:5
    d. *Summary:* Three Elements: Pray through the Lord's Prayer, Read one Chapter from the Word, Review a Memory Verse
    e. *Application:* Meet with the Lord for no less than 30 minutes each day and include the three elements in your meeting

F. **The Clothing of Jesus' Followers**
  1. **According to the Physical Birth:**
    a. *Learning Goal:* Recognize and confess inappropriate old habits and thought patterns, then adopt habits and thought patterns appropriate for a follower of Jesus.
    b. *Study* Ephesians 4:17-32 (using *Six Questions*)
    c. *Memory Verse: Ephesians 4:23-24*
    d. *Application:*
      1). List current habits and behaviors that violate Jesus' commands—unconfessed sins, lies and curses about yourself or others, use of magic, harmful relationships (corruption, binding/dependency

issues, etc.), customs, traditions and ancestral influence.

2). List new habits and behaviors that fit with Jesus' commands.

3). Pray together and confess your sins.

2. **Spiritual Characteristics**

a. *Learning Goal:* Recognize and confess secret sins

b. *Study* Matthew 6:25-34 (using *Six Questions*)

c. *Memory Verse:* Matthew 6:33

d. Application:

1). List the problems in your life that make you fearful of the future

2). Set priorities for the Lord to reign in your life and calm your fears

3). In daily time with the Lord, ask the Holy Spirit to fill and lead you

4). Pray with others

G. **Stand Firm (Power over Temptation)**

1. **Power over Temptation**

a. *Learning Goal:* Overcome trials and temptations

b. *Study* Matthew 4:1-11 (using *Six Questions*)

c. *Memory Verse:* James 4:7-8a

d. *Summary:* Four steps to conquer temptation: Submit, Resist, Pray and Celebrate

e. *Application:* When encountering trials:

1). Quote James 4:6-7

2). Submit to Jesus

3). Resist the tempter

4). Pray for assistance

5). Celebrate victory in Christ

2. **Spiritual Armor**

a. *Learning Goal:* Put on the spiritual armor

b. *Study* Ephesians 6:10-18 (using *Six Questions*)

c. *Memory Verse:* Ephesians 6:10-11

d. *Summary:* Draw a person wearing the Ephesians 6:10-18 armor

e. *Application:* Daily put on the armor, piece by piece

H. **Walk as a Follower of Jesus Christ**

1. **Walk in Faith**

a. *Learning Goal:* Take a step of faith

b. *Study* Matthew 14:22-33 (using *Six Questions*)

c. *Memory Verse:* Hebrews 11:6

        d. *Summary:* Teach with hand motions:
- 1). "Faith is not seeing then believing but believing then seeing."
- 2). "Faith is believing and doing what God has said, so it becomes reality."

        e. *Application:* Identify specific faith steps to be in the Lord's will

  2. **Surrender Oneself**

        a. *Learning Goal:* Minister to those in need

        b. *Study* Matthew John 13:3-17 (using *Six Questions*)

        c. *Memory Verse:* John 13:14

        d. *Summary:* Wash one another's feet as an example of humility.

        e. *Application:* Discuss how to serve others, and plan to do so.

I. Develop Personal Characteristics of a Jesus-Follower

  1. **Love**

        a. *Learning Goal:* Demonstrate love for others

        b. *Study* Matthew Luke 10:30-37 (using *Six Questions*)

        c. *Memory Verse:* Matthew 22:37-40

        d. *Summary:* Using hand motions, teach the great commandment: "Love the Lord with all of your heart, soul, mind and strength, and love your neighbor as yourself."

        e. *Application:* Ask the Holy Spirit to guide you in showing God's love to someone this week.

  2. **Hope**

        a. *Learning Goal:* Live with Hope

        b. *Study* Matthew John 11:1-44 (using *Six Questions*)

        c. *Memory Verse:* Romans 8:28

        d. *Summary:* Learn this quote:

        e. "God works all things for good: The bad becomes good, the difficult becomes doable and death leads to eternal life."

        f. *Application:* Discuss how Romans 8:28 applies to a time your prayer was not answered as you wanted.

J. Becoming a Spiritual Adult

  1. **Give**

        a. *Learning Goal:* Give an offering

        b. *Study* Matthew Mark 12:41-44 (using *Six Questions*)

        c. *Memory Verse:* 2 Corinthians 9:7

        d. *Summary:* Five characteristics of giving:

        e. (routine, joyful, sacrificial, tithe, blessing)

       f. *Application:* Commit to a sacrificial offering, then testify to how the Lord meets your needs.

   2. **Giving Birth to another New Church**

      a. *Learning Goal:* Help start a new group

      b. *Study* Matthew Acts 16:6-15 (using *Six Questions*)

      c. *Memory Verse:* Matthew 28:18-20

      d. *Summary:* Teach four ways churches were started in Acts:

         1). Church planters worked together

         2). Lay people started churches

         3). Churches started churches

         4). God called people directly to start churches

         5). *Application:* Choose five new people to share with from your Family, Friends and Acquaintances lists. Prepare with your group leader to pioneer a new group with some of these.

After the ten stages, most groups study Mark, then Acts.

Equip Churches and Leaders:

Church network teachers provide monthly teaching in the 3/3 training format. Foundational lessons emphasize both going and growing.

Send: Equip churches to send believers to new areas to repeat Plan A.

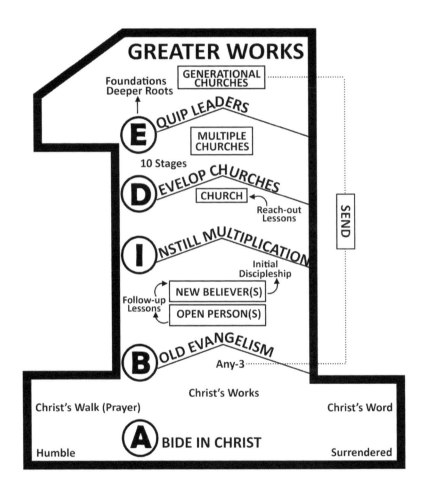

Appendix B:
First and Last Sacrifice Story

I know my sins are forgiven, not because I am a good person, although I do try to be good. I know my sins are forgiven, because God Himself already made a way for our sins to be forgiven.

Jesus Was Sinless

Jesus, the Word of God, was in Heaven with God from the beginning. Then Jesus was born into the world through the Virgin Mary. Even the Qur'an says this. Jesus never sinned. He once fasted 40 days and nights without eating anything. During this time, He was tempted in every way imaginable, yet He did not sin. He could overcome His passions, so He never married. He never killed anyone. He was born into a normal family (not rich or a religious hypocrite). He was an ordinary person like us.

Jesus Performed Great Miracles

He cast out demons, healed many people and He even raised the dead.

Jesus Prophesied His Death

It is interesting that, although Jesus was not old yet, He began prophesying to His followers, "I must die and will rise again." Do you know why Jesus said, "I must die?"

Why did Jesus have to die? (Adam and Eve Story)

The answer is in the books of the Law (Torah). The Law tells us about the first person, Adam, and his wife, Eve. In the beginning, God created Adam. From Adam's rib, God created Adam's wife, Eve. God put them in a perfect paradise, called the Garden of Eden. They were given the responsibility of taking care of the garden. They were also given great freedom to eat fruit from all the trees of the garden, except for the fruit of the tree of the knowledge of good and evil. God promised that if they ate that fruit, they would be punished severely—they would die.

Sin, Guilt, Shame, Fear = Leaves for Clothes

One day, the Devil (in the form of a serpent) tempted Eve to eat the fruit that God had forbidden. Eve ate from the fruit, then she gave it to Adam and he also ate from it. Suddenly, they were embarrassed and felt ashamed, so they made clothes from leaves to cover their nakedness. They were also afraid, so they hid from God.

Severe Punishment

Then God, who is all-knowing, came to them and brought severe punishment. Eve would have difficulty in childbirth, and until now, all women have that same problem. Adam would have difficulty working to make a living. And until now, all heads of households are in the same predicament. God cast Adam and Eve out of the garden like Paradise, and they could never return. Finally, they died. God's intention was for them to live forever, but because of sin, they had to die.

That is interesting, because as far as we know, Adam and Eve were responsible, good people; maybe better than us. We are not told in the Scripture, but perhaps they had already done thousands of good works. However, as far as we know, how many times did Adam and Eve sin before God judged them? Just one time, and that was a small sin. They hadn't killed anyone, committed adultery, or stolen anything. They merely ate a fruit which God told them not to eat. Sometimes we think that if we do more good things than bad things, that our sins will be forgiven, but that is not what the Bible says.

Promised Savior and New Clothes

After judging Adam and Eve, God also judged the serpent (Satan) who had deceived them. God promised that a Savior, whom He had anointed, would be born of a woman's seed, would defeat Satan, and would suffer to redeem people from their sins. Many prophets over a period of hundreds of years promised the coming savior, who would pay off our sin debt.

God still loved the people that He had created. So, He made a way for their sins to be forgiven. God did something interesting. He changed their clothes. Formerly, they wore leaves for clothes. Do you know what kind of clothes God gave them? God replaced their clothes with animal skins. It appears that God Himself offered the first sacrifice for the forgiveness of sins. The teaching of the Torah, Psalms, the prophets and the gospel is that if there is no shedding of blood, sins are not forgiven.

"That is Why Jesus Had to Die!"

All our forefathers offered blood sacrifices to have their sins forgiven: Adam and Eve, Abel, Noah, Abraham, Moses, David, etc. Then Jesus came, like I told you earlier. He was born of a virgin. That is interesting; Jesus was a woman's descendent. He lived sinlessly and performed great miracles. One day a prophet named John said this about Jesus, "Look, the Lamb of God, who takes away the sins of the world." That is interesting, isn't it? A person was called God's lamb. Why? Because a lamb is a sacrificial animal. That is why Jesus said, I must die." Jesus came to be God's sacrifice to pay off our sin debt. Therefore, Jesus surrendered Himself to evil people. They crucified Him, and His blood poured out. Before Jesus died, He said, "It is finished." Then He bowed His head and died. Our sin debt was paid off. Then Jesus came back alive on the 3rd day after His death. He appeared to His followers for 40 days, and then He was taken up into heaven. Someday Jesus will return to the earth as Judge of all people.

That is Why I Know My Sins Are Forgiven

The Bible tells us that if we surrender to Jesus as Lord and believe that He paid for our sins through His sacrifice and was raised from the dead, our sins will be forgiven. That is why I know my sins are forgiven.

Appendix C: Sample Lesson 1

Sanctification

Part 1: Positional Sanctification (Holiness)

I.   **Celebrate the Work**
   A.   **God's Big Vision:**
   B.   **Abiding in Christ:**
      1.   How did each trainee obey and teach the previous lesson?
      2.   To whom did those leaders teach the lesson?
   C.   **Doing the ABIDES Works:**
      1.   **Celebrate** each new generational group/church planted.
         a.   Who are they training to start new groups?
         b.   Who is the next generation training to start new groups?
      2.   **Map** new groups and progress of groups/churches in each network.
      3.   **Pray** for the struggles and advances of each trainee's ministry.

II. **Study the Word: Positional Holiness**
   A.   **Relevance:** Why must we know God's Word about being *declared* holy?
   B.   **Digging for Treasure:** What does the Bible say about *positional* holiness?
      1.   **Read** Revelation 4:5-8. Discuss what it means that God is "holy."
         a.   Note: "Holy" means "separate." God is "holy"—separate (far above) everything in all His qualities. He is pure and perfect.
         b.   "Why does the passage repeat God is 'holy, holy, holy'?"
      2.   **Review** the doctrine of God, using finger gestures (0, 1, 3 in 1).[45]
      3.   **Discuss** what each of these verses implies about God's holiness:
         a.   God is Light (1 John 1:5)
         b.   The Lord is a consuming fire (Heb. 12:29)
      4.   **Read** Romans 1:7. Discuss "Who are called 'saints' (holy ones)?"

---

45   Summarize Trinitarian doctrine with hand motions: '0' fingers for no Lord but God, '1' finger for only one God and '3' middle fingers together (not separated) showing God as the Father, Son and Holy Spirit.

      5. **Ask** "Why are all true followers of Christ called 'saints?'"

      6. **Read** Titus 3:3–7. Discuss:

         a. Does God consider Christ-followers holy because of good works?

         b. If not, what basis does God accept for considering us holy?

         c. How does this teaching differ from the trainees' old religion?

C. **The Gold Nugget (Conclusion):** God is holy and demands holiness. Positional sanctification occurs when a person repents, believes the gospel and receives Jesus as Lord. The person is then declared righteous by God and the Holy Spirit enters them. Their position as a "saint" is then secure. From that point the Holy Spirit also works to sanctify the person practically.

D. **Summary Lesson: Three Steps in the Sanctification Process**

      1. Declared holy positionally upon surrendering to Christ as Lord (regeneration)

      2. Made holy practically in living surrendered to Christ as Lord

      3. Made holy perfectly when meeting the Lord Jesus in Heaven

      Memory Verse: 1 Peter 1:16

III. **Send the Workers**

  A. **Plan Together**

      1. "How will you apply this lesson?"

      2. "To whom will you teach this lesson, and to whom will they teach it?"

  B. **Commissioning: Pray for and commission trainees to prepare others to abide in Christ and do the ABIDES works.**

Part 2: Practical and Perfect Sanctification (Holiness)

  I. **Celebrate the Work**

    A. **God's Big Vision:**

    B. **Abiding in Christ:**

      1. How did each trainee obey and teach the previous lesson?

      2. To whom did those leaders teach the lesson?

    C. **Doing the ABIDES Works:**

      1. **Celebrate** each new generational group/church planted.

         a. Who are they training to start new groups?

         b. Who is the next generation training to start new groups?

      2. **Map** new groups and progress of groups/churches in each network.

      3. **Pray** for the struggles and advances of each trainee's ministry.

II. **Study the Word: Practical and Perfect Holiness**
  A. **Relevance: Why must we know God's Word about becoming holy practically and perfectly?**
  B. **Digging for Treasure: What does the Bible say about** *practical and perfect* **holiness?**

Practical Holiness Occurs from Living surrendered to Lord Jesus

  1. **Read** 1 Thessalonians 4:1–8. Discuss:
      a. "What is God's will, according to verse 3?"
      b. "What must a Christ-follower do to be holy, according to verse 3?"
      c. "Besides adultery, what arouses lust and must be avoided?"
      d. List
  2. **Read** Galatians 5:16–25, then:
      a. List the fruit of the Spirit
      b. List the deeds of the flesh
      c. "What yields the fruit of the Spirit instead of the fruit of the flesh?"
  3. **Read** Hebrews 12:14–15. Discuss:
      a. Why is it essential to pursue holiness (verse 14)?
      b. How does God respond to those who aren't living holy lives?
  4. **Read** Hebrews 12:4–13. Discuss:
      a. What kind of discipline produces holiness?
      b. How do Christ-followers become holy?
  5. **Read** Romans 7:15, 21–25. Discuss your "new man's" desire for victory over your flesh (old man)
  6. Read Romans 6:8–14. Discuss these keys over temptation:
      a. Christ-followers have died Christ
      b. Christ-followers have risen with Christ
      c. Christ-followers submit to God rather than to fleshly desires

Perfect Holiness Occurs When We Meet Christ in Heaven

  7. **Read** Romans 8:28–30 and then 1 John 2:28-3:6. Discuss:
      a. Is it certain that every genuine Christ-follower will be sanctified perfectly?
      b. Compare this with what you grew up believing about heaven
      c. Contrast with views of heaven where man's lusts are satisfied

C. **The Gold Nugget (Conclusion):** The Holy Spirit begins at regeneration to help us live holy lives and guarantees that at death, we will be glorified. Glorification is perfect sanctification at death, when Christ-followers are united with Christ in heaven. Purification doesn't happen in hell or purgatory, as some teach. Hell is the final destination of Satan and his demons, shared by those who reject Christ's sacrifice.

D. **Summary Lesson:**
1. Positional sanctification occurs as we first surrender to Christ as Lord.
2. Practical sanctification develops as we live surrendered to Christ.
3. Perfect sanctification comes when we meet Christ in heaven.

   Memory Verse: 1 Peter 1:16

III. **Send the Workers**

A. **Plan Together**
1. "How will you apply this lesson?"
2. "To whom will you teach this lesson, and to whom will they teach it?"

B. **Commissioning: Pray for and commission trainees to prepare others to abide in Christ and do the ABIDES works.**

Appendix D: Sample Lesson 2

False Teachers & Teaching

Part 1: Identifying False Teachers & Teaching?

I.   **Celebrate the Work**
- A.   **God's Big Vision:**
- B.   **Abiding in Christ:**
  1. How did each trainee obey and teach the previous lesson?
  2. To whom did those leaders teach the lesson?
- C.   **Doing the ABIDES Works:**
  1. **Celebrate** each new generational group/church planted.
     - a.   Who are they training to start new groups?
     - b.   Who is the next generation training to start new groups?
  2. **Map** new groups and progress of groups/churches in each network.
  3. **Pray** for the struggles and advances of each trainee's ministry.

II.   **Study the Word: Identifying False Teachers & Teaching**
- A.   **Relevance:** Why is it important to know what has been revealed about False Teachers/Teaching?
- B.   **Digging for Treasure:** What has been revealed?
  1. **Read** Acts 20:28–32. Discuss: "What do we learn from this text?"
  2. **Read** Matthew 24:11. Discuss:
     - a.   What is said about prophets appearing after Jesus' time on earth?
     - b.   What is said about those adding to Scripture today?
     - c.   Note: The only prophets Jesus predicted are false prophets.
  3. **Read** Revelation 22:18–19. Discuss:
     - a.   What do we learn about the false teacher's view of Scripture?
     - b.   How is the false teacher's view different from the true teacher?
  4. **Read** 1 John 2:18–24; 4:1–4. Discuss:
     - a.   What do we learn about how false teachers regard Christ?
     - b.   How is this different from Christ's true identity?
  5. **Read** Galatians 1:6–10. Discuss:
     - a.   What do we learn about those who claim that salvation

requires something more than faith in the Lord Jesus Christ?

b. How do extra salvation requirements differ from the true way of salvation (Rom. 10:9–10)?

c. Note: Circumcision is one extra salvation requirement denounced in Scripture (Acts 15:1–2). A modern equivalent is the Jehovah's Witnesses teaching that, to be saved one must join their organization and follow their extra-biblical rules.

6. **Read** 2 Peter 2:1–3, 10. Discuss:

a. What do we learn about the character of false teachers?

b. How is this different from the character of true teachers?

C. **The Gold Nugget (Conclusion):** The Bible shows us how to identify false teachers and teaching through their teaching, character and actions.

D. **Summary Lesson:** Acronym: **FALSE**

1. Fake prophets arise

2. Add to and take away from Scripture

3. Lessen Christ's character

4. Salvation requirements added

5. Ethics that are hypocritical, sensual and overpowering

Memory Verse: Matthew 7:15

III. **Send the Workers**

A. **Plan Together**

1. How will you apply this lesson?"

2. "To whom will you teach this lesson, and to whom will they teach it?"

B. **Commissioning:** Pray for and commission trainees to prepare others to abide in Christ and do the ABIDES works.

Want to know more? Study the following verses:

F: Matthew 7:15–23
A: 2 Peter 1:16–21; Matthew 15:1–20; Acts 17:11
L: Colossians 2:8–10
S: Romans 3:19–25; Ephesians 2:8-10
E: Jude 4, 8, 10–16, 19

Part 2: Defense Against False Teachers & Teaching

I. **Celebrate the Work**
    A. **God's Big Vision:**
    B. **Abiding in Christ:**
        1. How did each trainee obey and teach the previous lesson?
        2. To whom did those leaders teach the lesson?
    C. **Doing the ABIDES Works:**
        1. Celebrate each new generational group/church planted.
            a. Who are they training to start new groups?
            b. Who is the next generation training to start new groups?
        2. **Map** new groups and progress of groups/churches in each network.
        3. **Pray** for the struggles and advances of each trainee's ministry.

II. **Study the Word: Defense Against False Teachers & Teaching**
    A. **Relevance:** Why is it important and helpful to know what has been revealed?
    B. **Digging for Treasure:** What has been revealed about defense against false teachers & teaching?
        1. **Read** Acts 20:28–32 and 2 John 8–11. Discuss:
            a. Why should followers of Christ be prepared for false teachers?
            b. How should believers deal with false teachers and teaching?
            c. How does this differ from our response to true teachers and teaching?
        2. **Read** Jude 3–4. Discuss:
            a. What kind of attitude should we have toward false teaching?
            b. How is this different from our attitude toward true teaching?
        3. **Read** Colossians 2:7–10. Discuss: How important is intimately knowing Christ and His Word to dealing with false teachers and false teaching?
        4. **Read** Jude 22–23. Discuss:
            a. How should we approach those deceived by false teaching?
            b. How is this different from approaching the false teacher? Why?
        5. **Read** 1 John 4:1-4. Discuss: What do we learn about responding to false teaching?

      C. **The Gold Nugget (Conclusion):** The Bible gives concrete ways to defend ourselves from false teachers and their teaching.

      D. **Summary Lesson:** The biblical plan for dealing with false teachers and teaching:

          1. Be on your guard for false teachers

          2. Warn false teachers with Scripture

          3. Aspire to intimately know Christ and His Word

          4. Rescue those who have been deceived

          5. Examine every teaching

        Memory Verse: Matthew 7:15

III.   **Send the Workers**

      A. **Plan Together**

          1. "How will you apply this lesson?"

          2. "To whom will you teach this lesson, and to whom will they teach it?"

      B. **Commissioning: Pray for and commission trainees to prepare others to abide in Christ and do the ABIDES works.**

Want to know more? Study the following verses:

Be: 2 Corinthians 11:1-4; 2 Timothy 2:14-18

W: 2 Corinthians 10:1-6; 1 Timothy 1:3-7

A: Ephesians 4:11-24; 2 Peter 3:14-18

R: 1 Corinthians 4:14-21; 2 Timothy 2:23-36

E: Matthew 4:1-11; Galatians 1:6-9